STRANGE
BUT
TRUE?

STRANGE
BUT
TRUE?

JENNY RANDLES & PETER HOUGH

LONDON NEW YORK SYDNEY TORONTO

PICTURE CREDITS

Permission to use copyright material is gratefully acknowledged to the following. BLACK AND WHITE ILLUSTRATIONS: *page 14 Daily Express; page 15 News of the World; page 16 The Times; page 22* Fortean Picture Library; *page 23* Steve Matthews/*Leighton Buzzard Observer; pages 25, 28, 30 and 31* Chris Robinson; *page 27* Dan Eldon; *page 36* Hiroshi Isobe/Life File; *page 38* (both) Penny Pellito; *page 52* Margaret Lupton; *page 54* Gary Havelock; *page 61* Fortean Picture Library; *pages 62 and 64* English Heritage Photographic Library; *page 68* Robin Laurence; *page 71* (map) Dick Vine; *page 73* Mark Oldroyd; *page 84* Ken Webster/Fortean Picture Library; *page 88 Wales on Sunday; page 90* Mark Oldroyd; *page 92* Maurice Grosse; *pages 95, 99, 102, 104, 105, 111* Mary Evans/Harry Price Collection, University of London; *page 98 Daily Mirror; page 100 Norwich Mercury; page 106 The Times; page 117* Dick Vine; *pages 119, 120* Colin Wright/BUFORA; *page 122* Mark Oldroyd; *page 123* Fortean Picture Library; *page 155* Rick Armstrong; *page 163* (top) Rick Armstrong, (bottom right) Dr Marge Rieder; *page 168* Mark Oldroyd; *page 171* Ron Bell; *page 179* Mary Evans Picture Library; *page 181* Fortean Picture Library; *page 185* Bruce Lampert. COLOUR ILLUSTRATIONS: *facing page 32* Reuters/Associated Press; *facing page 33* (top two) Bernard Lee/Calyx Photo Services; *facing page 64* English Heritage Photographic Library; *facing page 65* (both) English Heritage Photographic Library; *facing page 128* (above) Mary Evans Picture Library/Project Hessdalen, (below) Mary Evans Picture Library; *facing page 160* Bridgeman Art Library/Palazzo Ducale, Venice; *facing page 161* Bruce Lampert. Whilst every effort has been made to trace all copyright holders, the publishers apologise to any holders not acknowledged.

This edition published 1994
by BCA by arrangement with
Judy Piatkus (Publishers) Ltd

CN2828

Printed in Great Britain

CONTENTS

STRANGE
BUT
TRUE?

ACKNOWLEDGEMENTS

LWT Productions would like to thank all those who have helped in the making of *Strange But True?*

If you've ever undergone an experience, or have other evidence or theories on the unexplained which we may be interested in for future programmes, please write to:

Strange But True?
LWT Productions
The London Television Centre
Upper Ground
London SE1 9LT

Programme Credits
Research
Daniel Barraclough, Marie Ridonat, Rupert Smith, Edward Venner

USA Producer
Christine Scullion

Producer/Directors
Tracy Jeune, Cameron McAllister, Nigel Miller, John Morgan, Anne Ross Muir

Executive Producer
Simon Shaps

Editor
David Alpin

FOREWORD

WHEN I was a small boy, there used to be a programme on the wireless which was designed to astound and amaze the listener. It was called, I think, *Stranger Than Fiction*, and it was a collection of mind-boggling revelations of a scientific nature which, however impossible they seemed to be, were absolutely true.

I was always fairly unresponsive to stories of the supernatural and catalogues of unexplainable events. Too many people, it seemed to me, were ready to believe such things simply because they *wanted* to believe them. Our *Strange But True*? programmes tell stories which are strange in the extreme. Some you might find easy to dismiss as fanciful; others will impress you, if only for the sheer number of sensible down-to-earth witnesses who claim that what they describe really happened, and that they did not look for or necessarily welcome these experiences.

Every year, many thousands of people report ghostly presences, out-of-body experiences, lights in the sky . . . and the foreseeing of events that are so detailed in their accuracy that they cannot be put down to mere coincidence. I am ready to accept the first convincing explanation of a disturbing experience I once had. We had been filming the maiden voyage of an ocean liner, and I had asked one of the passengers to join me for some of the sequences – leaning over the rail, sharing a joke with the captain, that sort of thing. We were at sea for a week. When we got back to Britain, and before we went our separate ways, I reminded my 'co-star' of the date the film would be transmitted.

The next night I had a dream. My friend, dressed in a bright blue robe, was floating away into a background of total darkness and looking back over her shoulder with an expression of sadness and regret.

Some days later, when I went to the studios to record the commentary for the film, there was a letter waiting for me from her mother, telling me that her daughter had died of a brain tumour. I subsequently met the mother, and discovered that my friend had died on the night of my dream, and had been wearing her favourite blue nightdress.

Was it telepathy? A premonition? A coincidence?

Whatever the answer, I know that there are many thousands of people who could match my story with their own. An aunt of mine – and this is another story you won't find in this book – lived as a child in a large block of flats in London. One night she and her brother awoke, she tells us, to see an extraordinary apparition at the foot of their bed. It was dressed in a brilliantly-coloured outfit, and had hair drawn up into three huge points. They yelled, and the figure vanished. A week later they were taken to an exhibition of some sort and in the foyer they saw, in a glass case, the costume their nocturnal visitor had worn. It was the costume of the great clown Grimaldi. The name of the block of flats they lived in was ... Grimaldi House.

One final tale. During the making of *Strange But True?* we filmed a psychic at Dover Castle to see if he could detect the ghostly figures that several visitors had claimed to have witnessed. He wasn't able to single out any particular presence, but found a woman's name kept coming into his mind. Soon after, we had a phone call from the assistant manager at Dover Castle. He'd watched our filming and was cynical of the stories. But now he was quite shaken. An Australian tourist, who could not have known about the psychic, had just reported seeing a ghost – which gave her the very same name.

We invite you to become a paranormal detective as you peruse these accounts. Whatever your conclusions, may your own experiences, explainable or otherwise, be pleasant ones.

PSYCHIC AND HEALING POWERS

Human beings are the most remarkable products of four billion years of evolution. Not only are we possessed of extraordinary talents, as exemplified by great artists or musicians, but we seem to have fantastic potential within our brain. As yet knowledge does not encompass how anyone can heal the sick or resist all pain to a phenomenal degree, perhaps by drawing upon some hidden energy. Science has no easy answers for how the powers of the mind alone can see into the future and shape our destiny or help police solve baffling crimes. All that we can do is recognise that our consciousness is a vast, untapped store of seemingly limitless capacity and marvel at the wonders that result.

1
PSYCHIC CRIMEBUSTING

ONE of the most frequent criticisms made by sceptics about the paranormal is that it seems to be of such limited value. Dreams of trivial future incidents, a sense of knowing who might be on the other end of the telephone line before you pick up the receiver; these are commonly claimed psychic experiences. But they appear to have very little purpose. If some people really do possess amazing powers that the rest of us do not share, say the sceptics, then surely these skills could be applied for the benefit of all mankind in some positive and effective manner?

Psychic crimebusters challenge those very doubts: helping others is precisely what they profess to do. Ordinary people claim to have extraordinary talents which they can use in the field of amateur police work. They can adapt extra-sensory perception (ESP) and various other hidden gifts, such as dowsing, to seek out clues and new information that may point struggling detectives in the right direction.

Nella Jones is one such 'psychic crimebuster'. With her help, police forces all over Britain have been given clues unavailable by any normal means. Thanks to her aid countless frustrated detectives have solved crimes that defied all their routine investigations.

The police and psychic detection

As long as there have been police forces, there have been psychics willing to offer their assistance. John Alderson, former Chief Constable of Devon and Cornwall, has spoken about the phenomenal response that his force received to what was perhaps their most infamous case. In August 1978, schoolgirl Genette Tate disappeared while doing her newspaper delivery round.

Genette has never been found, but after Alderson indicated his need for help – of any kind – the frustrated detectives were swamped with calls from mediums and psychics who offered a wide assortment of sometimes conflicting evidence from their dreams and visions.

Alderson admits that, though this ploy was part of their 'strategy to detect', he and his officers did not treat the psychics' material on the same level as they treated hard information – it was merely used as a way to keep the case before the public eye, given the media's fascination with the paranormal. Although the police collated and recorded the dozens of visions that they received, they did not act upon any of them unless something came by way of more conventional techniques which suggested that it was important to listen to these psychic impressions.

One psychic crimebuster who assisted in the case was Bob Cracknell, an unorthodox soothsayer who has had numerous adventures with the police tracking violent crimes. From time to time he has been too accurate for his own good – police inevitably doubted that he could have obtained so much correct information by supernatural means.

Cracknell happened to be on holiday in the West Country when Genette Tate vanished. He offered some very specific information to the police – indeed, Cracknell is noted for being forthright and never fudges in his description of what he senses. He did succeed in describing a location which matched that of current police enquiries, but which was not public knowledge at the time. But he did not solve the mystery and was wrong when he insisted that the 'murderer' would be caught within a matter of days.

Roger Busby, public relations officer for the Devon and Cornwall force, was unimpressed by Cracknell but found the efforts of Dutch mystic Gerard Croiset rather more intriguing. 'That man,' he said, 'obviously could detect something from the environment.'

Croiset had a long reputation for helping police on the continent, and offered information about the Tate case simply by holding a pendulum over a map like a dowser and interpreting its response. He never even left his home town of Utrecht in Holland, but proved to be accurate in what he claimed. Later he was flown to Britain and provided further impressions that matched actual scenes from the schoolgirl's paper round. But he did not provide that vital missing clue.

HUNT FOR THE RIPPER

Between 1975 and 1980 Britain's biggest-ever manhunt was staged to try to find the so-called 'Yorkshire Ripper', a serial killer who murdered thirteen women in Northern England. Unsurprisingly, since normal police efforts were moving rather slowly, the psychic crimebusters were out in force.

Croiset was actively involved again, even locating the killer's alleged flat by dowsing aerial photographs. Famed medium Doris Stokes provided a pen portrait of the Ripper, care of her deceased contacts in the afterlife. This matched what Croiset had offered – both psychics felt that the murderer came from the north-east.

Doris Stokes provided many additional details which by chance matched those of a man who then lived in Sunderland. He found himself under so much pressure as a result of the medium's visions that he gave himself up to the police. The harassed man insisted that he was not guilty, but needed his name to be cleared so that his life could return to normal. He was indeed soon proven to be completely innocent.

This view that the killer originated from the north-east was based on anonymous taped messages received by the police in which a man with a 'Geordie' accent professed to be the killer. These misled almost everyone – including the psychics – for it turned out that the tapes had not been sent by the murderer. Indeed, when caught, it transpired that he was a local man from Bradford.

Only Nella Jones was uncannily successful in her visions. Before the Ripper was unmasked she went on record as stating that he came from Bradford. She described his house and the truck that he drove, gave a first name for him and stated that he had already been interviewed and released. She was correct in every one of these details.

Artful detective work

Nella was born half Romany and believes that this contributes to her amazing insights. She says: 'I see lots of things and hear and smell things too.' These describe images and scenes that she has never witnessed but about which she just seems to know. The visions spring up out of nowhere on the most unexpected occasions.

One Sunday Nella was doing the ironing. At the time she ran a cleaning company and weekends provided her with the only chance to catch up on her own housework. The TV news, on in the background, featured an item on the disappearance of a painting valued at £2 million from Kenwood House in London (see photographs opposite page 65). Nella describes her response:

'I saw a vision of the white front of this house. It suddenly came to me that of course they haven't found it. They've got the wrong place.' Somehow she knew these things and saw images dancing in her mind. She decided to put a call through to Scotland Yard.

Nella set aside her ironing and instinctively drew a sketch map on a piece of paper. Without consciously knowing why she was doing so, she then put two crosses on it.

> **THIEVES, swinging sledgehammers, smashed their way into an art gallery and escaped with a painting said to be worth nearly £2 million.**
>
> Last night a Europe-wide hunt was on for the gang who bludgeoned through the security network at K e n w o o d H o u s e, Hampstead, London.
>
> The raiders, who were in and out of the buildings within a minute, wasted no time in selecting their prize—"The Guitar Player," a seventeenth-century painting by the Dutch artist Jan Vermeer.
>
> The picture, of a girl, is so well known that experts regard it as too hot to handle. But the thieves might use it as a ransom lever.
>
> The gang whisked it away from a room that contained other art treasures, notably a Rembrandt self-portrait, valued at £1 million.
>
> They left the Rembrandt, perhaps because its size would have slowed their getaway. But the Vermeer was enough to make the haul one of the world's biggest art robberies.

The theft of the Vermeer created a huge stir. This extract, dated Monday 25 February 1974, comes from the **Daily Express**

By the time her phone call was directed through to Kenwood's local police station in Hampstead she knew what to say. Nella could describe the scene at the house, and how to walk from the back facade straight to the position of her crosses. One of these, she knew, was where the frame of the painting had been dumped by the burglars. This proved to be correct. The other was more difficult to identify, but she sensed it marked the position of a metal object connected with the theft.

The police were polite, but showed little desire to believe her. Nella says: 'They thought I was a nutcase. I was waiting for a little van to come and take me away. But shortly afterwards, when – as I now know – they had found the frame where I said it was, this very kind voice came on and said, "Would you mind coming to help us with our enquiries?"'

Detective Inspector Jim Bayes was the investigating officer who took her call. He remembers Nella's first approach and admits that many of his colleagues thought she was a crank. But, as they had no other leads to go on, the team decided to see what she could do for them.

The officers took her to Kenwood House where, armed with her notes and map, she had no hesitation in finding the precise location of the other cross. Says Jim Bayes: 'She didn't deviate. She went straight to the pond. It was as if she was drawn there. She appeared to be following her map. She said, "There is something very important in the pond in connection with the painting." And, while the rest of us were standing around wondering what to do next, Nella took off her shoes, hitched up her skirt and walked two or three yards into the pond. She bent down and came up with something – it was under a couple of feet of water.' To the amazement of the cynical policemen looking on, Nella had found part of the metal casing of the alarm system that had been attached to the back of the painting.

This was too much for some of the senior officers, and Bayes was ordered to treat Nella as a prime suspect for the robbery! But after questioning Nella thoroughly and discovering where she was at the time when the theft took

Nella at Kenwood, pointing to the spot where the frame was discovered

place they realised she could have had nothing to do with the crime and was a genuine psychic. Bayes added: 'I think in my heart I had known this all along, although my head said that she must be investigated thoroughly.'

HELPING THE POLICE WITH THEIR ENQUIRIES

Nella was adamant that she did not have a clue as to the nature of the object that she had found. She had simply known – without a moment's doubt – that it was something to do with the robbery.

She continued to offer information to the police. She told them that there would be several ransom notes from the thieves – and indeed there were. It emerged that the painting had been stolen by the IRA, and one note threatened that it would be destroyed on St Patrick's Day. But Nella reassured the worried owners that this was a bluff and would not be carried out.

Then Nella had a vision of where the painting was located. She carefully described a 'cavernous' area at a cemetery. Police thought that this might be nearby Highgate cemetery and Nella joined them in a bizarre nocturnal surveillance operation, but despite a major search of the area the painting was not found there. It seemed that the psychic had failed at the final hurdle, after successfully directing police to every other step along the way.

But Nella Jones had not been wrong. A few days later the painting was recovered from a cemetery a few miles away beside St Bartholomew's Hospital in London.

nothing is more lunatic than the fact that that thetheft á
the painting received more publicity, than the deaths of al
your soldiers;

Of course we have not contacted anyone associated with the

I.r.a they could not orgnise a piss up in a brewery;

the price sisters have given no sign of gratitude all we

have established is that a capitalist society values its

treasures more than humanity

therefore we will carry our lunacy to its utmost extent
the painting will be burnt on st patrcks night with much
coverting about in thetrue lunatic fashion;

our av...

*Part of the ransom letter received by **The Times** which threatened to burn the painting*

A PROLIFIC CAREER

The discovery of the stolen Vermeer painting and the clues to the identity of the Yorkshire Ripper are by no means Nella's only successes. She has had an astonishing career.

In July 1974 Nella suddenly had a vision set in an antique shop in Brighton, a town that she barely knew. Viewing the scene as if she were floating 'out of body' by the ceiling, she watched in horror as a man and a woman, both drunk or drugged, argued in the presence of a second man who came to them up the stairs. The first man was stabbed, after beating the woman senseless, and the second man got a can of paraffin and set the shop ablaze.

Without a moment's hesitation Nella knew this was a real tragedy that was – or would be – occurring and had to warn the police. She called Scotland Yard, who tried to identify the shop by questioning Nella further. They checked several premises in the town, but Brighton has dozens of similar establishments. In the end they had to let the enquiry lapse.

However, on 24 September 1974 – two months after her frightening vision – Brighton beat officer James Martin came upon an antiques shop that was on fire in the early hours of the morning. Investigation revealed that the blaze had been started deliberately and that the bodies of a man and a women lay in the flat above. The man was a drug addict and had been stabbed in the back and the drunken woman had been assaulted. Despite a massive man-hunt the shop owner, wanted for questioning about the crime, was never traced. Even Nella was unable to use her powers to say where he had gone.

In another murder case Nella amazed police officers by re-enacting previously unknown details of how a woman was killed when they took her to the scene of the crime. She felt herself being attacked from behind and tumbling down the stairway, grabbing on to the bannisters before crashing to the floor. She was correct in these and many other aspects and then gave investigating detectives the correct make and colour of the murderer's car, as seen in her vision and verified later when this man was arrested and sent to trial.

After encountering evidence such as this, one leading CID officer stated coolly that he had to believe what Nella Jones told him, adding: 'If she told me there was a body buried under the wicket at Lords, I'd have no hesitation in digging up the pitch.'

More often than not such bold statements from police officers are offered anonymously, but in November 1992 when Detective Constable Neil Pratt retired from the police he was very willing to endorse Nella's value to his work.

He spoke of an investigation he once made into the brutal slaying of a young woman in Telegraph Hill Park, south London. He had taken Nella to the park and as they walked along one of many pathways she stopped immediately and pointed to the exact spot where the crime had been committed, although this was far from obvious given the surroundings. She also identified a place where physical evidence had been dropped by the killer as he jumped a fence and ran away. She was proved correct in this assertion.

However, at present British courts will not accept evidence from a psychic and many British police officers do not want to risk the stigma of admitting to psychic assistance. Some in fact accuse psychics of being 'people watchers' who use psychology to make reasoned guesses about situations. In Nella's case, however, the police are genuinely impressed and say it is a mark of her ability that they turn to her for help, 'time and time again'.

METROPOLITAN POLICE SERVICE
International and Organised
Crime Branch,
New Scotland Yard
Broadway
London SW1H 0BG
Telephone 071-230 1212

You have given a great deal of assistance to the Police Service over the years and it has been our pleasure to express our gratitude to you.

I know that some police may have seemed sceptical of your abilities in the past (as a group police officers are trained to be so) but it is a mark of abilities that police turn to you for help, time and time again.

We all appreciate that your information cannot be given in a court of law but your insights have proved to be invaluable in directing our lines of enquiry in many cases.

I hope that your assistance through our unique relationship can continue for many years to come.

An extract from a letter which Nella received from the Metropolitan Police

SNIFFING OUT THE CLUES

One unusual method often used by psychic crimebusters is psychometry – which involves holding an object that recently belonged to a missing person or which might have been directly involved in a crime. This seems to act as a catalyst and triggers the flow of mental images.

Cheshire clinical psychologist Dr John Dale has trained himself to perform this technique, utilising his own latent extra-sensory perception. He does not believe that psychics are biologically different from anybody else, and so felt there was no reason why he should not be able to do what they claimed they could do.

Dr Dale receives an object – perhaps a coat worn by a missing girl, or a weapon found at the site of an abduction. Holding these, he tries to empty his mind and images flood in. He says: 'The problems start with the act of translation. I am receiving emotions and feelings and these are being turned into pictures in my head. I can be wrong just as often as I am right.' He warns that it is easy to let your own beliefs creep in.

Other experiments conducted by Dr Dale, under the auspices of Manchester University psychologist Dr John Shaw, involved 'reading' the contents of sealed envelopes from twenty different people, each containing a personal item. On about six occasions he scored hits in describing emotions or scenes linked to the objects.

Dr Dale has successfully aided several police forces in Britain and has received letters acknowledging his assistance. However, he has maintained a low profile and has no interest in self-publicity.

The way ahead

In the USA the use of psychic crimebusters is now a common occurrence. Police forces are well used to receiving aid from mystics and visionaries.

In December 1980 the disappearance of nurse Melanie Uribe from the hills to the east of Los Angeles made the headlines. When young mother Etta Smith heard the story on the news she instantly had a vision, similar to others that she had experienced in the past. Just as in Nella's case, she was engaged in household chores at the time when the images swamped her senses. Without a moment's hesitation Etta knew the missing nurse was dead. She could see her white-clad body dumped in a desert canyon.

Feeling that it was the only decent thing to do, Etta drove to the investigating police station and told detective Lee Ryan her story. On a map she located the area where the body must be – Lopez Canyon.

Etta left the police precinct unconvinced that the authorities believed her and would act upon what she had told them. So, once back home, she bundled her two young children into the car and all three of them set off for the desert.

Following her instincts, Etta drove straight to the spot where she just knew the murdered nurse must be. Immediately she spotted a flash of white in the sun and went closer on foot to make sure, then panicked and fled from the scene. On the way back they met a police patrol, so Etta took them to the site where they recovered the woman's body.

Thinking that this awful nightmare was at last over, Etta returned home. But barely an hour had passed before she was escorted back to the precinct to 'help police with their investigation'.

It soon became obvious that they could not accept her story about a psychic vision. She had been far too accurate, even describing the clothing worn by the nurse, which was not her normal uniform. In the early hours of the following morning they asked Etta to take a lie-detector test. The polygraph operator urged the police officers to postpone the test for a few hours, because Etta was by now far too tired and emotionally drained and as a result the machine could give a false reading. But Etta wanted it over with and knew that she had nothing to hide.

The test results were inconclusive. But to her horror, the reluctant psychic crimebuster was now informed that she was going to be arrested on a charge of murder!

Etta Smith was in fact never charged, but was held in custody for four days. In the meantime police had established that Melanie Uribe had been set upon by three men who had raped her before killing her. The police knew much of this even while they were holding Etta without charge.

In March 1987 Etta became the first psychic to sue the police for damages because of their false accusations against her. Detective Lee Ryan and the polygraph operator both testified on her behalf, and she successfully convinced the Los Angeles court that she had merely attempted to do her duty as a patriotic citizen by reporting what she knew – even if she had not the faintest idea how she came to know it! The court awarded Etta more than $26,000 in damages.

This case provides a timely warning for all psychic crimebusters, but it will not stop them from trying to help solve crimes. And as Nella Jones and Etta Smith demonstrate, police forces the world over are sitting up and taking notice of this extraordinary source of information.

2
VISIONS OF
TOMORROW

WHEN Chris Robinson goes to bed at night he steps into a time machine. In his dreams he sees the future set out in terrifying detail.

Chris has had many frightening experiences. He has seen tomorrow unfold before his eyes. The worst part for him is to sit helpless, as disaster looms, knowing that he has seen it coming, that he has tried to warn others, but that all too often he has not seen enough to make a difference.

Chris has premonitions. His mind scans ahead of itself and grabs a small piece of tomorrow. As the forty-three-year-old Bedfordshire man emerges into the harsh light of day these visions are still there – shimmering before him, but fast disappearing like flakes of melting snow. He tries to hold on, like a fisherman hauling in a slippery catch – hoping that this time he can make sense of what he sees before the images are lost. Praying that for once he may be able to use his gift to help save a life.

A history of the future

Mankind has always had visions which appear to foretell the future. The Bible is filled with stories of prophetic dreams, and most civilisations have similar legends.

Many religious prophets saw the future by way of their dreams. The visions of Elijah, Mohammed and others were revered by the culture of their day, which saw them as a direct link between earth and heaven. Tribal societies, such as those of Africa and Australia, have shamans or medicine men, specially selected because of their frequent claims that they dream about the future. Western society too has its shamans.

One of the most famous dreamers was a sixteenth-century doctor named Michel de Nostredame, better known as Nostradamus, whose published predictions describing the entire future of the world have never been out of print. They are constantly being reinterpreted in the light of modern historical events, but he is credited with foreseeing the Great Fire of London, Napoleon and World War II. Opinion on the validity of the predictions is strongly divided, but their continuing fascination is unquestioned.

Nostradamus, the famous sixteenth-century 'dreamer'

In October 1966 a rain-swollen coal tip collapsed on to a school packed with children at Aberfan in Wales. The tragedy was the subject of intense investigation by psychic researchers: afterwards, dozens of dreams were collated that appear to have foreseen the event. Just before the disaster one of the victims had drawn a picture of a black mass covering her school and told her parents that she was not afraid to die, as she would be with two named friends. A few days later she was buried next to these same children in a communal grave.

Paranormal researchers have found that major tragedies trigger more dreams of the future than any other type of event, probably because of the strong emotions involved – emotions being the most common form of precognition. Studies into the sinking of the *Titanic* in 1912, the assassination of President John F. Kennedy in 1963 and the destruction of the NASA space shuttle *Challenger* in 1986 have firmly established this pattern.

COINCIDENCE OR GENUINE PREMONITION?

Scientists who seek to comprehend the nature of time and space face a major problem. Dreams are usually fleeting experiences, often incomprehensible to the waking mind. If they seem to predict the future it may be an illusion, for the spectre of coincidence is always present. Dr Keith Hearne, an expert in premonitions research, explains: 'Statistics show that there is one major plane crash in the world somewhere every two weeks. So a premonition about a plane crash has to be very specific for me to be interested in it.'

Chris Robinson's story is different. His dreams are frighteningly specific. They are also frequent and have much evidence to support them. To him the future is really out there, waiting to be unravelled. Yet we still do not know if we can change our fate or whether we are doomed to follow the script, come what may.

'Dreaming true'

Chris's dreams started to come into their own in 1989 and he says he was very frightened by them. Eventually, he began to share his visions with other people. As those visions became reality he now had independent support, which at least made things easier for him to accept. If he was crazy, he felt, then so were all those people who were having similar experiences. Since he

Chris Robinson working at his computer

23

knew that the others were perfectly sane and normal, he argued, then so were the visions.

Chris came to know whenever he had a dream that might foresee the future: 'I dream like everybody else. It's a mixture of pictures which you can recognise as being reality and pictures which really could not exist. The dream has a backdrop – a forest, city, housing estate or whatever, but there are things which do not fit into these normal scenes … I see symbols and these symbols have specific meanings.'

DREAM SYMBOLS AND THEIR MEANINGS

Psychiatrists and psychologists such as Jung and Freud discovered a century ago that most dreams use symbolism to obscure their meaning. This complicates research into visions that may foresee the future, particularly as each person's dream imagery is personal to themselves.

Chris Robinson has composed a dictionary of the symbols within his own dreams to help him interpret his visions. These symbols include:

- *Ticking clocks:* an explosive device with a timing mechanism
- *Dogs:* terrorists
- *Fish* imply that any terrorists or criminals in the dream will be caught
- *Snowfalls* enhance the threat, meaning that any scene foretold may be imminent

Chris can also decipher postcodes and names from his dreams. If, for example, a BT telephone engineer's van appears in his dream, it usually means the event will happen in Belfast – BT being that city's postcode.

When Chris realised that he was 'dreaming true' he decided to approach the authorities. Before long he was so sure he had a mission to carry out that he bombarded the local police and others with details of his dreams. When the events that he described in many cases actually came true, the recipients of his warnings had no choice but to believe him.

THE TERRORIST ATTACK

One of his first major successes came in May 1990 when Chris began to dream that he was in Stanmore, Middlesex. He was always beside an RAF base. Then he visualised dogs. Eventually his dreams became very explicit, with the dogs scrambling through a graveyard, clambering over a fence, turning into people, placing a ticking clock in the grounds of the RAF base and being surrounded by photographic equipment.

Chris decided that terrorists were going to mount an attack and rang the air base to warn those in charge. The voice on the end of the line listened intently, but could promise no action. However, an entry was made in the station log to confirm that this call had been made.

Chris was not satisfied, for by now his dreams about the terrorists had become very powerful. He decided to drive to the base to confront the security police in person.

On his way to Stanmore he was unsure exactly how to convince the military: 'You can't really explain what it feels like to *know* that something is going to happen. I was frightened. I was nervous. But I knew that if I did not go there and warn them, there could be a lot of people killed.'

Brian Earl, the security police sergeant at the base, had spoken with Chris

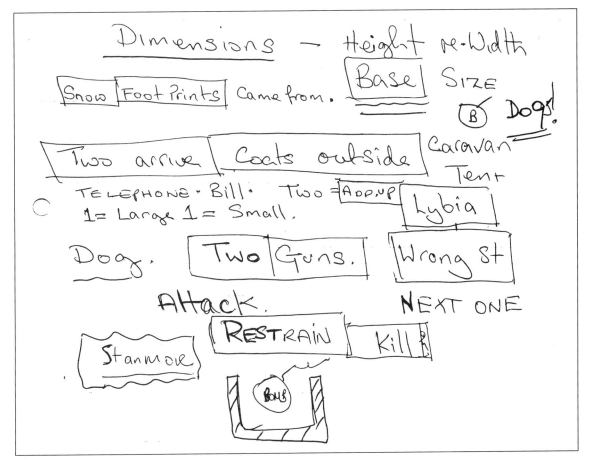

A page from Chris's diary predicting the attack at Stanmore

on the phone the night before. He had already established that the man was not a crank, having called a senior police officer to whom Chris had reported some earlier dreams. Earl said: 'As a precautionary measure we contacted the Bedfordshire police, and they confirmed that he was known to them and, in the past, had assisted them through his dreams.'

When Chris Robinson arrived at the base an hour or so later Brian Earl led him to an interview room. Chris had brought records proving that various earlier dreams had come true, and described in depth the forthcoming raid on the base as he had seen it in his dreams.

Earl notes: 'He said he saw a vehicle, yellow and green with some RAF personnel sitting inside, and two stationary aircraft. He was very agitated, because he seemed so intent on getting the message over. He came across as very sincere, but what impressed me more than anything was that he had travelled down at his own expense to try to warn us. It was quite obvious that he believed in what he was doing.' The security sergeant was in fact so impressed that he briefed the station commander and the guard was doubled for a week after Chris's visit.

Unfortunately, Chris would not offer any precise dates for the timing of his vision and the guard was restored to normal when nothing happened. But four weeks afterwards a group of terrorists did indeed attack. They entered, just as in Chris's dream, through a graveyard at the rear of the complex, planted a bomb and wrecked the unit's photographic stores. Luckily nobody was injured.

DEATH IN AFRICA

During the next two or three years the Bedfordshire police regularly received faxes and phone calls from Chris Robinson. Sergeant Richard McGregor in Luton confirms that he is a designated contact, and that the police try to filter something useful out of the material with which Chris supplies them.

However, in May 1993 Chris had a dream in which he saw a man and a woman surrounded by bees. He knew by now how to unravel this image, and he realised that it would be of little use to his Bedfordshire contacts. It meant someone in Africa engulfed by a local mob. He also sensed danger.

The next day Chris went to a party and met Kathy Eldon, an American woman living in London. Only after he mentioned his dream did she explain that her son (pictured opposite page 32) was a photographer working in Africa. Indeed, twenty-two-year-old Dan Eldon was a brilliant news photographer, then in Somalia, whose pictures had appeared in prestigious publications such as *Time* and *Newsweek*.

Kathy Eldon says that when Chris discussed his dream with her she felt no threat for her son, because 'Dan was so streetwise, had been brought up in

One of the photographs taken during Dan's time in Somalia. A young Somali boy helps his family move to a safe neighbourhood in Mogadishu

Africa and was a friend of everyone'. In addition, she knew that no journalists had been killed in Somalia up to that time.

However, this response did not allay Chris's fears and he was concerned enough to travel to Mrs Eldon's flat and plead further with her. She recalls him saying: 'Please just warn him to be very careful.'

But the sense of tension would not go away. By early July the dreams had returned. They included more bees, photographic lenses and salt water, and again stressed that danger was imminent.

On the 10th Chris had his most vivid dream so far: 'It was like a reality dream, you're actually there watching a scene. There were people being chased ... it was somewhere near the sea. Four people were going to be murdered and they all had cameras, so I assumed they were photographers.'

The next day he warned a close friend of Kathy Eldon's, hoping to figure out exactly what he was foreseeing in his still confusing dreams. There were yet more images: 'Thugs ... gangs ... people needing help ... no one can see me ... Nikon f. 4 ... rescue me ... Kathy.' These were among the most precise images that he had ever seen, and he knew that he had a route directly to the mother of one of the victims. But even that was not destined to prove effective.

On 12 July, Dan Eldon and three other photographers were killed in Mogadishu on the coast, attacked by a crowd in circumstances that chillingly mirror the details in Chris Robinson's dream. Nearly all the imagery that he saw before the event from his location thousands of miles from the tragedy fits perfectly with what actually transpired. For example, a Nikon f. 4 was the type of camera lens Dan was using. Some of the details that Chris had warned about, such as how one of the four murdered photographers had a

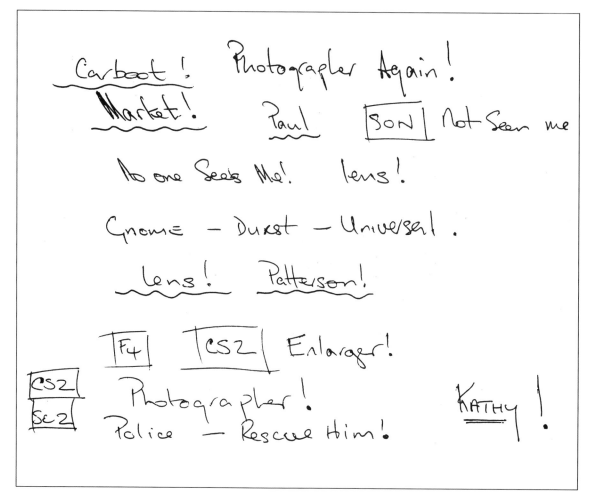

An extract from Chris's diary containing more warnings for Kathy

heart attack as he fled from the mob, only emerged weeks later when the autopsy results were released.

Dan Eldon's death had a terrible effect on Chris's confidence. When he saw the news report on TV he knew instantly that one of the victims was the same man whom he had only ever met within his dreams. Chris broke down and wept in despair. He says: 'It was all there and we didn't stop it. I felt that I'd failed. There had been concise messages in the dreams which were saying what was going to happen, and we didn't do enough, or we didn't do the right things, or maybe I didn't go to bed early enough and I missed something which would have been vital.'

Of course, even if the exact time and place of coming events had been seen in advance, Chris Robinson has no need to reproach himself. There is no evidence to suggest that these men's deaths could have been prevented. Their fate may have been sealed whatever action anyone had taken.

CAN THE FUTURE BE PREVENTED?

American psychic researcher William Cox conducted an experiment based on passenger trains that were involved in major accidents. He found a clear tendency for passenger numbers to fall from their normal level for each journey that was fated to end in disaster. Researchers suggest that people dreaming of the crash ahead of time subconsciously motivate themselves not to take that particular trip, even if they fail to remember their dreams.

In May 1979 David Booth from Cincinnati had a series of dreams about a horrific air crash, and contacted the local office of the Federal Aviation Administration. Booth was able to describe the type of aircraft, its colour, the airline involved and many other specific details that he saw night after night.

The authorities took him seriously but could do little, since Booth was unable to say where or when the accident would occur and they could not possibly ground every flight, even from a single airline. Just over a week after Booth's dreams began, an airliner departing from Chicago's O'Hare airport lost an engine and plunged to earth in a ball of flame. Nobody on board survived.

However, two passengers booked to take the flight cancelled at the airport, seemingly as a result of a premonition. Those passengers were well-known actress Lindsay Wagner and her mother. So it would seem that even if future events themselves cannot be prevented, individuals may subconsciously ensure that they are not participants.

TWO ROCKETS ... TWO CROWNS

Within a matter of days of this terrible experience, strange dreams were haunting Chris's sleep once again. On 16 July he called his police contact, Detective Sergeant Richard McGregor.

McGregor recalls that conversation: 'His dreams are more like cryptic clues in a crossword. He told me there were two boxes of fireworks, and he took that as a clue that there were going to be two explosions. One of the boxes was open, and from that box there were two rockets. Once lit they went into the air and collided above. He then described what he thought were like crowns coming down and said he was close enough to virtually catch them.'

The following week Chris became more convinced than ever that something terrible was imminent, as the dreams were now so vivid. He had also sketched what he had seen on a page in his dream diary (see opposite), which he always kept beside his bed and filled with notes and pictures of whatever images, voices and messages he received. The colliding rockets were like jet aircraft, while the crowns resembled descending parachutes, although he did initially wonder if they meant something to do with a crown court.

When Chris awoke on Saturday, 24 July he felt certain that he had to act

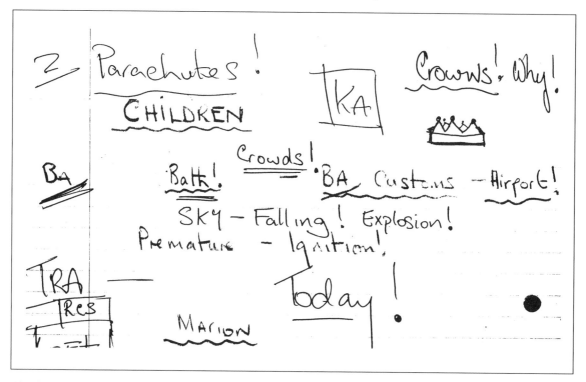

Chris's dreams, as this extract shows, were becoming increasingly specific

that day. But he still could not decode his confusing dreams. So he called newspaper astrologer Penny Thornton, who kept her own dream diary. He had spoken with Penny before, after discovering their mutual interest in this field; perhaps she might provide the missing link.

Penny Thornton recalls that she and Chris talked about a dream of her own from the previous night, which contained an image of the letters SLR on a car number plate. She guessed it meant a single lens reflex camera. As they chatted, an airshow was being promoted on the TV, which happened to be on in the background at Chris's home. The final piece fell into place. He knew he must 'act as a camera' and record that event.

The airshow was many miles away, at Fairford in Gloucestershire. Chris set off straightaway, but it took him several hours to drive there and it was around 3pm when he arrived.

Chris drove along a little lane and stopped close to the airfield where a police patrolman was parked. He tried to get into the show, explaining his predicament. But the display was already well underway and the gates were closed. However, a small group of people were leaning on a fence looking out across the field and Chris joined them. Two Russian MiG 29 jet fighters were swooping through the air above the packed spectators, giving an extraordinary low-level aerial display.

The 'crown' sketches

Chris knew what was now inevitable. Within minutes of his arrival the two planes collided wing to wing: the scene was captured live by cameras and screened on news bulletins around the world. The pictures (see opposite page 33) show two fire-breathing 'rockets' crashing into one another in mid-air and exploding into flames, then smashing into the ground just beyond a screaming crowd of thousands. It was a near catastrophe.

The little group of onlookers surrounding Chris Robinson by the gate stared at the unfolding holocaust in utter horror. 'My God!' said one. 'Nobody can survive that.' But Chris said quietly in reply: 'Don't worry. In my dream they come out on their parachutes. There's no problem.'

And he was right. Through the billowing smoke two parachutes, the 'crowns' of his dreams fell smoothly to earth. Both Russian pilots had a miraculous escape.

As the crowds drifted away, still shell-shocked by what they had seen, Chris was smiling inwardly. But he was also bemused: 'I was at the right place at the right time, but how did I know in advance? The pilots didn't.'

He found a phone and put through a call to Detective Sergeant McGregor in Luton. The officer recalls Chris's exact words: 'You'll never guess where I am,' followed by an explanation. It was all so obvious now. Everything that the psychic had said on the phone the previous week suddenly made sense.

The policeman admits that he was 'amazed and really a bit stunned' by this dramatic sequel to the man's dreams. He says that he does not generally believe in such matters, but notes: 'I cannot get away from the fact that Chris Robinson went to that air display, and what he told me on the phone a few days before was basically what happened on that Saturday.'

Nor is there any doubt that Chris was at Fairford. The *News of the World* quoted him as an eye-witness in their report of the accident the next day.

Communications with another dimension?

Dr Keith Hearne makes it clear that proper studies are needed if science is to progress, but after assessing Chris's dream diary he said he found the results 'beyond coincidence'. He adds: 'I am very impressed with Chris Robinson's abilities. There are many convincing cases. He certainly comes up with some very unexpected predictions – things that you wouldn't expect to happen, and these interest me because they are not trivial things.' And because Chris's dreams are recorded in advance, this makes them more amenable to scientific verification than those of his historical predecessors, which in turn makes them much more valuable as evidence suggesting that we can foretell the future.

But what does Chris think is the source of his visions? He believes that he sees so much tragedy because dead police officers are communicating these visions from another dimension; one to which we may all graduate after death. These friendly contacts are trying to stop some terrible things from happening.

After Dan Eldon died, Chris claims to have received further dreams inspired by the photographer. The murdered man sent messages for his family that specified where to trace some missing photographic negatives, and indicated his desire to launch an African charity in his name. This was, indeed, subsequently set up.

Kathy Eldon is clearly impressed. She admits that at first she had to consider whether she was just in a particularly vulnerable situation, yearning for evidence that her son lived on. But she says of the material Chris communicated: 'Most people did not know about it. A lot of the stuff has never been published. I think I have to take it all very seriously.' As for her overall opinion: 'Chris is a remarkable fellow. He is generous with his dreams and only wants to help people. He has helped our family immensely.'

Facing: *Dan Eldon with a group of smiling Somali youngsters*

Can we 'dream true'?

Research suggests that everyone may dream of the future from time to time, but most people forget the details of their dream as soon as they wake up. As a result if these abilities do exist, they are rarely discovered. Evidence from parapsychologists indicates that as many as one in three dream scenes may incorporate imagery ahead of time, although perhaps it will be heavily symbolised and difficult to interpret.

Their experiments involve groups of people keeping dream diaries. They are told to wake as slowly as possible, and focus on the first image that comes into their mind as they return to consciousness. They are advised not to open their eyes or move about, but work around the images that they see. These first impressions should result in a clearer memory of many of their dream scenes from the night before.

Then they can find out if they are just ordinary dreams, or something more...

Facing: *Dramatic pictures of the plane crash at RAF Fairford in Gloucestershire*

3
PSYCHIC POWERS
ON TRIAL

W E KNOW that some people have the ability to subdue pain without the use of medication or anaesthetics. But could that control extend to major operations which include the removal of bone? If so, would it be linked to self-hypnosis, the release of endorphins (the body's natural painkillers) or psychic powers? When Penny Pellito claimed she lost her pain-blocking psychic powers after an accident in a DIY store, she decided to take the company to court and sue. Penny wanted compensation not just for her physical injuries, but for the loss of her psychic powers too.

Body control

Mind over matter works. Certain individuals can slow down their heartbeat by will, control pain through acupuncture and expose themselves to fire without ill-effect. This has been scientifically investigated and documented, although some aspects remain controversial. A depressed state of mind can make us ill, so why not the contrary? Can a positive attitude be so advanced it can control body function and protect it from injury and even death?

CONTROLLING INVOLUNTARY FUNCTIONS

Adepts of yoga can control their body functions to a fine degree. In a famous case, one yogi was able to change the temperature of two areas of skin just a few inches apart by a difference of 10 degrees Fahrenheit. Experiments at an American hospital demonstrated that subjects in states of transcendental meditation were skilled in controlling heart rate, blood pressure and the electrical resistance of the skin.

The conscious control of involuntary body functions is also achieved by practitioners of Zen, a Japanese form of Buddhism, and occurs during trance states experienced by members of certain African cults. These functions can be slowed down so much that the subject is almost in a state of suspended animation. Experiments have been carried out in which people who can do this have been buried for several days without ill-effects.

ACUPUNCTURE

Until recent years acupuncture was deemed as nothing but mumbo jumbo by the Western medical establishment. Now doctors are referring patients to registered acupuncturists. This Chinese system of inserting needles into particular areas of skin to prevent disease supposedly works by manipulating energy lines circulating around the body.

It has been used most effectively in the West as an efficacy for anaesthesia. Patients have elected to have acupuncture rather than drugs before major operations. Scientists have tried to rationalize the phenomenon by claiming the system releases endorphins, 'the brain's natural opium'. But while acupuncture removes pain, it does not numb the body as traditional anaesthetics do. Patients are aware of every cut but feel no pain.

OPERATION IN CHINA

In 1971 western journalists were invited to Beijing to observe a series of major operations carried out without anaesthesia. *Sunday Times* journalist Neville Maxwell watched as one patient had a thin steel needle inserted into his right forearm. This, apparently, numbed the whole chest area and allowed a procedure to commence which involved the removal of a tubercular lung. While this took place, the man was fully conscious and chatted with theatre staff.

After the operation the wound was closed and the needle removed. The man was helped up and his arm massaged. He showed no evidence of discomfort. Indeed, immediately afterwards he gave a press conference. Since that time, these operations have become more widespread.

FIRE WALKING

During the phenomenon of fire walking, not only is pain suppressed, but the walker suffers no injuries. For thousands of years shamans or medicine men of certain primitive religions have demonstrated an ability to walk across a pit of blazing hot coals or stones. In recent years it has been demonstrated that almost anyone in a positive state of mind can fire walk.

During the 1980s Professor Carlo Fonseka, a physiologist at the University of Colombo in Sri Lanka, attended many fire walkings in his country to find a rational solution. He discovered that most fire beds were less than 18 feet long, and walkers stepped across in just a few seconds. When he did tests on the feet of experienced walkers he discovered that their soles were thicker than normal because they did not wear shoes, and were therefore more resistant to heat. When he persuaded volunteers to walk across a bed of coals, those with softer feet had to move faster!

However, can this be the full explanation? Anyone who has put a hand near a well-lit barbecue knows that even to touch it briefly would cause injury. The consequences of walking across barbecue coals, even fleetingly, are obvious. Indeed, some walkers, thick-soled or not, have suffered terrible injuries. *So why are some immune from pain and injury?*

Fire walking at the Takao Festival in Japan

Fire walking, like acupuncture and body function control, seems to demonstrate a phenomenon that is beyond scientific understanding. Is that power already within us, or is it channelled through from outside?

Operation Penny

Penny Pellito is a larger-than-life American, who for many years claims to have had at her disposal psychic powers which she describes as being channelled through her. Chief of these is the ability to block out pain. This is no whimsical airy-fairy claim, but has been verified by the medical profession and recorded on video film.

Penny first realised she was special at the age of seven, and assumed that everyone shared her gift. 'I fell down on a rock in a park and suddenly I didn't feel the pain.' As a child she could only control pain for short periods, but as she grew older she could sustain this ability for longer and had more control over it. Eventually Penny realised that she had the power to remain pain-free around the clock. All she had to do was switch on to 'automatic'.

'It was like being ten years old again, not feeling the arthritis in my hands, not feeling it in my spine. When something dropped on my foot, I felt *it* and not the pain.'

But being pain-free had inherent dangers – for instance, she would be totally unaware of the onset of a heart attack. So Penny rarely went into 'automatic'. Instead she would 'switch' her powers on and off. The first time she really put them to the test was during a minor operation.

A MINOR CYST

Dr Harry Pepe has been the Pellito family's doctor since the mid-1970s. When Penny complained of a small cyst on her arm, Dr Pepe agreed to remove it in case it became malignant. As he filled a hyperdermic with local anaesthetic, Penny told him she did not need it. Dr Pepe insisted but she was adamant, so he told her to lie down, disinfected the area, and held the scalpel ready to cut. He had serious doubts about going ahead, but since Penny was absolutely insistent he made an incision and cleansed it; still she didn't move.

Penny kept talking to Dr Pepe to put *his* mind at rest. He removed the cyst and then sewed up the wound. The doctor was impressed, but he knew there were people who could withstand the pain of a minor operation. At that stage he did not understand that the issue was not pain threshold, but a total *lack* of pain.

Penny Pellito aged seven, when she first realised she had a special gift, and, right, after her foot operation

At the beginning of 1985, after an injury sustained when a deer stepped on her foot which left her unable to walk, Dr Pepe referred Penny to a specialist called Dr Sheldon Willens. There was a cyst on the bottom of her left foot, and Dr Willens decided it had to be cut out. Penny agreed, but told him not to give her any anaesthetic. Dr Willens was not too happy because he knew the operation would be a painful one. But, like Dr Pepe, he found he did not need to give his patient an anaesthetic.

A MAJOR OPERATION

Removing the cyst, however, did not cure the problem. Penny's foot was still painful, and four months later the cyst had grown back. Dr Willens examined her foot again, and commented: 'These little cysts are caused by pressure from the bone inside the foot. The problem was with the fifth metatarsal head. I explained to her we were going to have to open up the foot and actually cut out this bone. I told her again about anaesthetic, but she said she didn't need it. I said you will definitely need it – I've not heard of anybody ever having a bone cut without anaesthetic!'

He was very apprehensive and consulted Dr Pepe, who agreed that the operation could not be done in this way. Dr Willens told Penny of his decision but she was adamant, and finally he gave in, getting her to sign a form which absolved him of responsibility. On the day of the operation Dr Willens prepared for surgery while office staff looked on. As she lay ready for the operation, Dr Willens, who had become sleepless with worry, had one last try to change her mind. He failed.

Dr Willens described the procedure that he now followed: 'I took a knife and opened up her skin and she didn't bat an eyelash. I spread the tissues and applied retractors. Then I used scissors and got down to the area where the bone was, and moved the tendon off to the side. After exposing the bone I cut into the area surrounding it to free it. All the time she was joking with my staff. I'd never seen anything like it in my life.'

But the best was yet to come. Dr Willens had to cut off the bone. For this he used an oscillating saw.

'It makes a racket – not as much as a chainsaw, but real noisy. You could cut through a shankbone of beef with it. I took that segment of bone out and left the toe intact. Then I sewed it up inside and outside and dressed it. I just could not believe it. The level of pain when you cut through the periasteum

A reconstruction of Penny's successful foot surgery

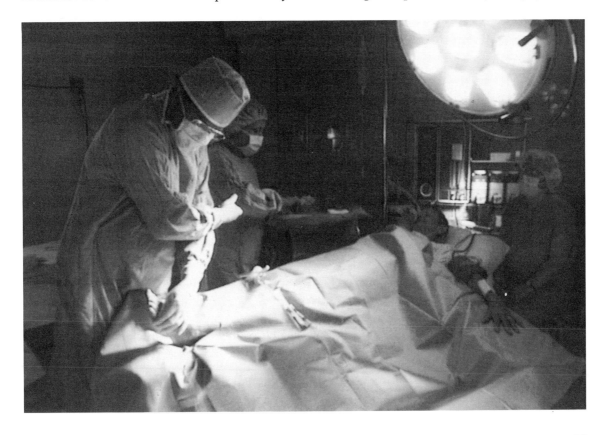

bone is excruciating! Yet the whole time Penny was lively, waving her hands around. It was a once-in-a-lifetime experience for me. I've been practising foot surgery since 1959, and I've never seen anything like it before.'

Penny Pellito's next operation was to be filmed and later presented as evidence in a court of law. Yet even before anything was diagnosed, Penny says she *knew* through her powers of extra sensory perception that she would have a lump in her right breast.

At that time Dr Allan Fields had just done a hernia repair on her husband. Penny asked him if he could remove a lump from her breast some time in the future, and do it without anaesthetic. He agreed, but afterwards Penny discovered he was only humouring her. Once again she had an uphill struggle.

About two years later she had a mammogram which showed a lump. Penny told Dr Pepe that Dr Fields had agreed to operate on her. Dr Pepe and Dr Willens helped persuade Dr Fields that it could be done without anaesthetic, but the hospital refused permission, so the operation was performed at Dr Pepe's surgery. A camera crew was present as Penny lay on the bed prepared for surgery.

Dr Fields described Penny's reaction during surgery as 'phenomenal'. 'As a matter of fact she was kind of joyous. The only time I was apprehensive was when I first used the scalpel. Everyone knows what it's like to be cut by a piece of paper, so imagine what it is like to have an incision with a scalpel – it would be agony. Breast tissue is a very sensitive part of the body. Yet she chatted to the television crew as if she was lying on a beach.'

A void inside

Disaster struck when Penny was helping her husband recover from a heart attack. Part of his rehabilitation programme included building raised flower beds in their garden. They went to a DIY store to buy some wood and were lifting out some boards from a low shelf when three boards came crashing down on Penny's head. Aside from the physical pain endured, Penny described feeling 'a void inside of me'.

Two weeks later she went ahead with surgery which was already scheduled to remove cysts on both wrists and one on her right breast – all without anaesthetic. 'When I was in surgery I began to feel the void growing stronger. Towards the end I began to experience feelings I shouldn't have. When the nurse put a cast on my arm I felt the heat of it setting. I shouldn't have felt it.'

At home her hands began to swell and her fingers looked like fat sausages.

Blood came through the bandages. She asked her husband for some ice. When he discovered she was suffering, he yelled: 'Go on automatic, stop the pain!' But she could not do it. Dr Pepe had to saw off part of the cast to relieve the swelling.

'By this time,' said Penny sadly, 'I realised that the ability was lost. It never came back, and I had to attribute it to the lumber hitting me on the head.'

GOING TO COURT

Penny decided to take the DIY store to court, seeking compensation for her physical injuries *and* the loss of her powers. It was a case which made legal history – no one had ever sued for loss of psychic ability before.

A few days before the trial, the store offered $17,000 in an out-of-court settlement. Penny turned it down because, she says: 'I wanted to legally prove that something – no matter what anybody wants to call it – did exist.'

In court, the doctors who had performed all seven of her operations gave evidence. To show what Penny had gone through, Dr Willens demonstrated the oscillating saw used to cut the bone from her toe. The bone itself, preserved in a jar, was presented to the jury. Jurors also watched the videotape taken during Penny's breast operation.

But in the end, the $2,000 in damages they awarded Penny was only for her physical injuries, not her loss of psychic powers. And with medical and legal bills totalling well over $20,000, it felt like she had lost badly.

Until, that is, she read newspaper reports in which the jurors were interviewed. One of them was Harry Weintraub. He says: 'I had no doubt whatsoever that she had some ability to block pain. Her case fell apart due to the fact she had had another operation two weeks after the incident. She didn't really prove she had lost her talents. I was truly convinced she had some amazing powers.'

What was Penny's secret?

No one who had witnessed Penny's operations doubted that she was able to block pain. But what was the mechanism behind her apparent powers?

HYPNOSIS?

A psychiatrist called Dr Charles Mutter was asked by the DIY store's lawyer for an independent opinion on whether or not Penny had psychic powers. Dr Mutter is a past president of the American Society of Clinical Hypnosis, and has taught hypnosis to physicians, dentists and mental health specialists. Dr Mutter's findings, as presented to the court, show that he had no doubts of the source of her 'powers'.

'It was clear to me that she was using self-hypnotic techniques. She was very gifted at this as well, because she could do it very quickly and spontaneously. She would go into a trance and as a result turn off sensation to any part of her body. Some people do not close their eyes in this state, and can even communicate to others. This was not psychic power, just hypnotic technique.'

The doctors and surgeons who had attended her did not agree with Dr Mutter. Dr Fields had studied hypnosis for the alleviation of pain in post-operative cancer patients. He said: 'It's interesting that in order for these people to become self-hypnotised there was some sort of mechanism involved. The classic one is a swinging watch or counting backwards until the individual is programmed. Penny did none of these things. There was no trance, she didn't concentrate on anything, she was absolutely natural. Was she using hypnosis? The answer is no.'

Dr Willens concurred: 'I studied hypnosis in training, and most people in a hypnotic state are quiet, more somnambulant. They lie back and don't ask too many questions. Penny was joking and wanted to sit up.'

DRUGS?

Could Penny have been using drugs? Not according to Dr Willens: 'I don't think so. Anything that would have dulled the pain would probably have dulled her brain as well, and she didn't appear to be drugged in any way.'

Dr Pepe was more vociferous: 'No, she couldn't have used drugs because she wouldn't have been alert. It would have been plain she was under sedation. The thought processes wouldn't have been clear. She did not have any painkillers or sedatives, and if she had had an anaesthetic she would have been sleeping.'

Dr Fields agreed, pointing out that there were no classic symptoms such as constricted pupils, reduced salivation or changes in posture. Could Penny have applied a local anaesthetic? His investigations ruled that out. 'There was no evidence of any kind of puncture wound. However, we do use an air pressure device for vaccinating children, which leaves no mark. But what we see when we cut into the tissue is a swelling, a water-type infiltration of the fluid. Apart from its physical presence we would see changes such as clotting of blood. Penny had none of these.'

Even more important, when a biopsy was performed on the tissues removed during her breast operation nothing was found that would indicate the presence of drugs.

A MEDICAL CONDITION?

Was there a medical condition to explain the phenomenon? Dr Fields, Dr Willens and Dr Pepe were all unanimous that there was no known medical condition to explain an ability to block out pain at will.

PSYCHIC POWERS?

Penny Pellito never had any doubts right from being a child: the gifts were paranormal, and they were channelled through her from outside. Her head was like a radio receiver. The accident had damaged it, and the signal could no longer get through. Penny herself called it a 'pipeline' in which came psychic gifts. But while her claims of pain-blocking powers grabbed the headlines, her other 'powers' went largely unnoticed.

Penny's abilities had increased with age. At their peak she never had to take any sort of medication, and forgot what it was like to have a headache. She was able to lift enormous weights, and immediately after the operation on her foot did seven hours of housework. The pipeline worked both ways. Through it she was able to 'pipe out' the pain, reduce swelling and heal much more quickly than other people. Penny hoped that the doctors and psychiatrists would be able to discover how her gift worked so that others could learn to do the same; this would be highly beneficial, for example, to high-risk heart patients who are often unable to have complicated surgery because of the dangers of giving them an anaesthetic. If the need for an anaesthetic was eradicated, they could go ahead with life-saving surgery.

Penny was able to predict things, too, and perhaps even make them happen. She knew that Dr Willens liked to gamble sometimes and decided to reward him after the foot surgery. 'When Dr Willens went to Las Vegas I told him that I would give him the capability to make him a winner.'

Dr Willens confirmed this: 'She told me there would be a very short time frame when I won. There was a period, maybe an evening or an afternoon, when it seemed I knew what every card was coming up next. For instance, I was sitting at the table playing blackjack and I had about 2,000 dollars in front of me. Up until then I had been betting maybe one hundred to two hundred dollars.

'The dealer asked if I wanted to bet. It was like I didn't know what I was doing. I usually wouldn't bet that kind of money. I put down all the chips, and sure enough, I had a blackjack. I can't describe how it felt, but if I needed an eight, the next card was an eight. It was like magic – but it didn't last long enough, unfortunately!'

What then did Dr Willens think was the source of Penny's abilities? 'I don't know what she had. I don't know if it's psychic abilities or a gift from some place. When my daughter in Seattle had a back problem her doctors wanted to carry out some procedures. I spoke to Penny about it, and she said: "Don't let them do those things, she'll be fine in three or four months" – and she was. When my granddaughter was born with an eye problem, a paediatric ophthalmologist said she would have to wear glasses and needed surgery. Penny said: "Six months and she'll be fine." She was, and she still is – four years later.'

Penny Pellito's case was scientifically tested by qualified doctors in a laboratory environment. Her abilities were demonstrated not just once, but many times, and recorded for posterity on videotape. Further, the sceptics' explanations were met and successfully challenged. Although the court would not finally admit that Penny had lost her powers, to Penny and those close to her, they were very real.

'Now I live like everyone else and it hurts,' she says. 'It hurts because I know when I die I'm going to feel great pain. This shouldn't be. The anger has never stopped, and neither has the hurt.'

4
THE
INVISIBLE TOUCH

IS THE acceptance of psychic healing by western medical practitioners about to take a great leap forward? In recent years homeopathy and other forms of alternative medicine have slowly begun to infiltrate mainstream medical practice. Doctors who once would have dismissed claims of 'miraculous' healing are coming to believe that some of these cures represent more than just the power of suggestion. But how long might it be before healers are part of a medical practice, working side by side with conventional doctors? Five or ten years at the earliest? In fact a healer has been working at the Bridge Street Surgery in Otley, Yorkshire, since 1990 ... with startling results.

What is spiritual healing?

Psychic or spiritual healing usually involves the laying on of hands, through which the healer is said to direct healing energy to the patient. This is not, many believe, the practitioner's own energy – rather, it is an energy channelled through from 'elsewhere'. People often describe feeling an intense heat. Most healers do not actually touch the patient, but move their hands around or above the afflicted area. The hands also act as a diagnostic tool, supposedly communicating to the healer the area of disharmony. Members of the National Federation of Spiritual Healers, founded in 1955, are prevented by their code of conduct from carrying out actual diagnosis.

ALTERED CONSCIOUSNESS

Healers believe that the body has seven major energy centres known as 'chakras'. Blockages in these cause disharmony and therefore illness. Practitioners use their abilities to unblock the centres, allowing the healing process to start.

Some believe that they are awakening the patient's own mind, enabling it to heal the host body by tapping into the aura, or etheric double, allegedly surrounding the physical body. The first stage is to create a positive attitude in the patient. Chronically ill people are naturally depressed, 'encouraging' the illness to prosper.

A centuries-old tradition

Healing without recourse to medical assistance has a long history in many cultures. Often there have been religious overtones: in societies such as those of ancient Greece and Egypt, for instance, the priests were also healers – possibly because all illness was seen as divine punishment. Both the Egyptian Imhotep and the Greek Asklepios, patron saint of physicians, had the greatly valued gift of healing, and both were believed to be able to heal through their dreams.

The Eastern religions have always been convinced of the power of spiritual healing, and this belief still forms a major part of many of their philosophies and martial art forms. In India, China, Tibet and elsewhere body and soul (or mind, body and spirit) are inseparable, as they once were in the West.

Jesus Christ is perhaps the best and most obvious example of a healer in the history of mankind. The miracles described in the New Testament include cases of healing which cannot be explained in any rational way. Again, illness at this time was regarded as something not of this world – the work of the Devil. By defeating illness through such extraordinary means, Jesus could demonstrate the power of good over evil.

But the great powers of healers were feared as well as revered: after the first few centuries AD, healers began to be regarded with suspicion and associated with occult practices. Undoubtedly fakers and charlatans did exist – and still do; but from that time the emphasis in healing, particularly in the West, moved to medicines, drugs and more invasive methods such as surgery. Only now, in the late twentieth century, is the West gradually moving to a position where ancient, and yet seemingly novel, forms of healing can once again be treated seriously by more than a small minority.

Modern healing in practice

Lorraine Ham was already a successful healer when Dr Geoffrey Hall of the Bridge Street Surgery in Otley became interested in her. She had been working with cancer patients at Cookridge Hospital in Leeds.

BREAKING DOWN THE BARRIERS

The breakthrough from the monopoly of orthodox medicine to a reconsideration of spiritual healing was greatly assisted by three movements: Theosophy, Christian Science and Spiritualism.

- **The Theosophical Society**, founded by Madame Blavatsky in the late nineteenth century, aimed to blend Western and Eastern ideas of sickness and to bring back the spiritual element which had been lost.
- **The Christian Science movement**, founded in America in 1875 by Mary Baker Eddy, proposed that all illness was in the mind. Material things, Christian Scientists consider, are meaningless, and only the spirit has any importance. They reject conventional medical treatment and feel that people can heal themselves through faith in God.
- **Spiritualists** hold that healing energy is channelled through to sick people by spirit guides who have no visible or tangible form. Contact with these spirit guides is made through seances.

Elements of all three movements occur in most modern psychic healing.

At the outset, Dr Hall knew very little about 'natural' healing, as Lorraine calls it, and what he did understand made him sceptical. But a colleague talked him into meeting some healers she was using in her hospital practice, and when he saw them he felt that several did indeed have special qualities. After doing some research into complementary medicine he came to the conclusion that it was an effective form of treatment. What particularly impressed Dr Hall was that sick animals had shown improvement after being subjected to healing. Obviously no animal could be psychologically influenced in the same way that a human being might, which ruled out the placebo effect and other psychological explanations.

BEYOND CONVENTIONAL MEDICINE

When Dr Hall first spoke to his partners about inviting a healer to join the practice he was surprised that his senior colleagues were receptive, and that the initial scepticism came from the younger ones. After meeting Lorraine Ham for the first time, he said, 'I only had to sit and talk with her for several minutes, and I felt more relaxed, better.' She accepted his invitation to join the practice in 1990.

Patients are sent to Lorraine in exactly the same way as those referred to any specialist. The doctor writes a referral letter to her, and after she has seen the patient she sends an initial report with a treatment plan. When the treatment is finished she compiles a final report and asks the patient to come back and see the doctor who made the initial referral.

Dr Hall says that the patients Lorraine sees are those whom traditional medicine cannot help. 'When I was a student I was taught all the things that Western medicine can do, and like most doctors I've learnt by long and sometimes bitter experience all the things it *can't* do. Sometimes we reach the limit of Western medical technology, yet we know help is still needed. Those are the kind of patients we are referring to Lorraine.'

He admits he does not fully understand how Lorraine's treatment works. 'I find that some of the things Lorraine does clash with my scientific training. But I'm frequently working with Western medical treatments that I don't fully understand. I may prescribe a drug, and although I understand its effect, I don't know exactly *how* those effects are achieved.'

The practice partners send Lorraine almost all their patients with long-term chronic physical diseases, which often include emotional complications. 'Lorraine seems to achieve particularly good results with this group,' says Dr Hall. 'I have been surprised at what she's been able to do. She's been far more successful than I anticipated. Approximately 80 per cent of all people who are referred to her feel they have benefited, and many have been greatly improved by her treatment.' Even in cases where the disease is still active, the victim's attitude towards it changes, and they find it easier to cope.

Inherited powers?

Lorraine Ham's great-great-grandfather, Te Hau-Takiri Wharepapa, was a Maori chief who came to England from New Zealand in the late nineteenth century with a party of other chiefs to meet Queen Victoria. Wharepapa was also a *tahunga* – a skilled healer using natural plant medicines. Lorraine's grandmother was a healer too, and so is her cousin. Lorraine believes healing ability might be genetic.

She first discovered she had healing powers around 1980. Another healer told Lorraine she could sense it in her, and was amazed that she had not realised it herself. The healer explained that when Lorraine was ready to accept the gift, things would start to happen. She thought about it almost every day for the next three months, then suddenly decided it was the right thing to do.

A PRECOGNITIVE VISION

The first time Lorraine performed any healing she had already seen it happen in a vision. 'When I see things, it's a bit like watching them on a

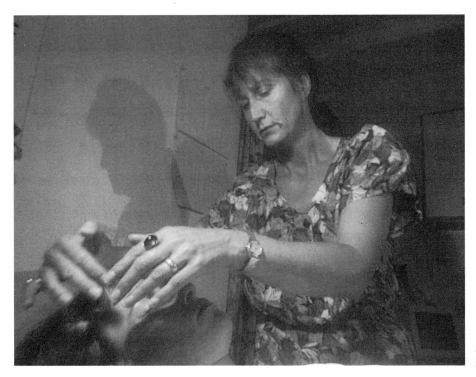

Lorraine Ham
treating a patient

television screen. They're before my eyes but also in my head.' When she met a woman with a hand spasm, she knew her from the vision she had had the previous day. The woman could not open her hand, but Lorraine *knew* she could help her. 'I explained I was just going to hold her hand, and apologised at the same time, feeling quite foolish. She let me hold it, explaining it wouldn't open. As she was talking I was opening her fingers.' As the woman marvelled at her now mobile hand, Lorraine felt embarrassed and walked away.

RELAXATION AND CONTROL

Over the years Lorraine developed her healing skills and more recently refined the procedures necessary for an orthodox medical practice. When a patient visits her for the first time, a consultation takes place to build up a case history. At the same time Lorraine picks up 'energies' from them that help her make an assessment of the illness and decide on the treatment. She often starts with relaxation exercises, and assures patients that they are in complete control of the situation.

'Some people are quite vulnerable when they're sick, so it is important they know that at any time they can speak or move around. At the end of the session I usually ask them how they felt during the healing, and they often describe different sensations. Some just feel relaxed, others describe heat, gentle warmth, coolness, cold or tingling sensations.'

If 'contact' or hand healing take place she usually starts at the head, where she picks up a deeper insight into the problem. Her hands then wander over the body around the chakras, sensing energy depletions and blockages which she sets about balancing and unblocking. Every case is different, however, and treated on its own merits. Sometimes Lorraine empathises with the suffering of the patient. 'If someone's in pain I sometimes feel it. When people are emotionally upset I can often sense what's wrong before they tell me.' That is what apparently happened when she met Susan Simpson.

Curing phobias

When Susan Simpson was pregnant with her first child she experienced a terrifying reaction when she went out in the car with her husband. Whenever the car came up to a traffic island surrounded by heavy traffic Susan would panic and curl up, whimpering. She sweated profusely, felt terrible and shouted at her bemused husband.

What was the cause of this mind-numbing fear? Was she just being over-protective of her unborn child, or was there something more? Susan had never been in a car crash. The phobia disappeared once the child was born, but when she became pregnant again it resurfaced.

Susan sought medical help, but her doctor found he could do nothing for her and was reluctant to prescribe tranquillisers because of her condition. Instead he referred her to Lorraine. Susan was Lorraine Ham's first patient in her new job at the surgery.

PAST-LIFE TRAUMA?

Lorraine went through the procedures and carried out some healing. Afterwards, she decided to tell Susan of a feeling which had been troubling her – a story about a heavily pregnant woman driver who had been involved in a fatal car accident at a traffic island. Susan identified with the scenario immediately. 'I explained to Lorraine that she had just described something which had been in the back of my mind all the time.'

Lorraine believed that Susan was still holding on to the trauma of a car crash from a past life, and told her: 'This belongs to another time and you can let it go now. It's gone and you don't need to hang on to that energy anymore.'

Although it took a few weeks for the fear to disappear entirely, after the session she immediately felt better about getting into the car and confidently drove home. Susan Simpson was cured of her phobia.

Life from a barren land

Margaret Lupton came to Lorraine with stress-related problems connected to work. During one of the sessions Margaret mentioned she had been trying to conceive for almost ten years.

When Margaret married, she and her husband Peter decided to try for a family after a couple of years. After five months with no results she went to see the doctor. He told her to continue for a year, and after that time she returned for further advice. The doctor told Margaret to keep temperature charts so that the couple could attempt to conceive at the optimum times, but twelve months later she was still not pregnant.

When she was sent to a specialist he explored the family background and decided that the couple ought to wait a little longer for nature to take its course. Still nothing happened, so over the next four years Margaret and Peter underwent various tests and internal procedures at Bradford Royal Infirmary.

These tests found no physical abnormalities of Margaret's uterus or the ovaries, and Peter's sperm count was normal. The hospital offered Margaret a course of hormone treatment, but after the first painful injection the couple decided enough was enough. They would accept life without children and enjoy it to the full. So they began to spend money more freely on clothes, restaurants and exotic holidays. The pressure was off, they were able to settle into a more enjoyable lifestyle, and Margaret concentrated on her career as a teacher.

VISUALISATION AND AFFIRMATION

Margaret now started attending relaxation classes run by Lorraine, which led to private treatment for work-related stress. Eventually she opened up about the years of failure attempting to have children. From then on Lorraine concentrated her healing efforts around Margaret's abdomen, and gave her some tasks to carry out at home. These were visualisation exercises and verbal affirmations designed to promote a positive state of mind.

All this time Margaret never told Peter what she was doing in case she raised false hopes in him. As the summer approached, the couple were looking forward to a holiday touring Malaysia. Then, although she had none of the normal signs of pregnancy, Margaret felt something was different. The day before they were due to leave she got the results of a pregnancy test. It was positive. When she told Peter the news he was elated. Then they worried about going away, but their doctor pointed out it was still early days and there was no real reason to cancel the holiday. The first thing Margaret did

Margaret Lupton with her two children, Joshua and baby Rhys

when they reached their destination was send Lorraine Ham a postcard telling her the news.

DISTANT HEALING

On the couple's return Margaret began to lose the baby. She was confined to bed, and Lorraine carried out several sessions of healing down the telephone. According to Lorraine: 'Distant healing involves focussing on that person and bringing healing energies to them through thought.' The therapy worked, and Margaret Lupton gave birth to a boy, Joshua, in 1989. The couple were subsequently able to have another baby in 1992.

More than psychology?

Although the healing of animals rules out a total psychological explanation for healing, psychology does seem to play a part – especially where there does not appear to be a physical reason for a problem. The relaxation techniques used by Lorraine Ham verge on hypnosis. Patients are put into an altered state of consciousness which perhaps makes them more receptive to healing.

In the case of Susan Simpson and Margaret Lupton sceptics could say there is no need to resort to the paranormal – psychology can provide the answers. But is it as simple as that?

Speed

Gary Havelock, a champion speedway rider, was racing in Poland when he was involved in a crash. One of the Polish riders lost control and went into the back of his bike, ramming him into the safety fence at high speed. Gary went over the handlebars and somersaulted down the track.

He was severely bruised, with deep gashes to his shoulder and his right hand was broken. At the hospital the Polish doctor told him he would have to take six weeks off racing to allow the bones to knit back together. Gary was appalled: he had the Commonwealth Final coming up at Kings Lynn in nine days' time.

A GRIPPING SITUATION

Back in England he saw a physiotherapist who examined his injured hand and also said it would be weeks before he could ride again. The biggest problem was the lack of grip. But Gary had to ride in the Commonwealth Final if he was to qualify for the 1992 speedway World Championships.

It was then that Gary's girlfriend suggested he went to see Lorraine Ham, who had already helped her with several problems. Gary was quite sceptical, but he was desperate and felt he had nothing to lose.

Not much progress was made at the first session: afterwards Gary's hand still could not grip and was still very painful. When he arrived for the second appointment, just four days before the race, Lorraine rubbed his fingers for a while and talked to him. Then she positioned one of her hands above and the other beneath Gary's injured hand, without actually touching it, and began moving them around. 'As I worked on Gary's hand,' she said, 'I had the sensation that the bones were actually knitting together. At that point I knew he was going to be healed.'

Gary felt something too: 'It was like somebody had a blow-torch or heat-lamp on my hand. Afterwards when she actually touched me her fingers were icy cold.' The hand felt instantly better, and over the next few days it improved rapidly. According to Gary: 'When it came to race day, it wasn't 100 per cent, but it was certainly a lot better than it would have been without the treatment.' He came third at the meeting. 'To do that nine days after breaking some bones in my hand was quite amazing.'

Champion Speedway rider, Gary Havelock

Gary Havelock's fast-healing hand persuaded other riders to seek out Lorraine Ham's services, and there was an added reward to come. Gary went on to win the World Championships.

The healing presence

One morning in 1989 the Revd Alan Kitchen woke up in agony: there was a terrible pain in his neck and down his arm which prevented him moving them. Somehow he managed to get into his car, and Anne, his wife, drove him to hospital where he was put in traction for ten days. Then they sent him home, put him on painkillers and told him to rest in bed. Alan was still in a lot of discomfort and a special orthopaedic bed was ordered for him.

The Revd Alan Kitchen

Lorraine Ham was a family friend, so they decided to ask her for help. She came and carried out some healing, but according to Alan it made little difference. The pain moved a bit, but after she had left it was just as bad. However when Lorraine returned to carry out further healing, things began to happen.

A HEALING CRISIS

She spent several hours healing Alan, and during most of that time Anne was in the room with them. After relaxing him, Lorraine began to move her hands over his body. Although she never actually touched Alan, the pain built up until it became so intense he had to ask for a break before continuing. Lorraine described it as 'a healing crisis, similar to a boil bursting before it can get better'.

After a few moments she carried on, and once again the pain began to increase. Then, suddenly, everything changed. Alan explained what happened: 'Things began to happen that I've never really come to terms with. The atmosphere in the room seemed to change. What she was doing changed. A tremendous sense of warmth, love and peace flooded the bedroom. I didn't quite get up and walk, but I wasn't far off.

'At the end of the session we were all in tears, and Anne and Lorraine were hugging. In twenty years of ministry I've never come across anything like that. Something incredible happened. If you asked me to describe a miracle I couldn't describe it better. The following day I was able to walk around and resume my work, and I've not had any neck problems since.' Anne concurred with what happened: 'The feeling in that room was indescribable. We all felt it, a presence, spreading love.'

The orthopaedic bed was due for delivery the following day. Alan took great delight in cancelling it.

The future

What future does healing have in relation to traditional Western medical practice? Perhaps the comments of Dr Hall's colleagues are symptomatic of a general change of attitude in the profession. Dr John Baldwin explained that medicine was already adopting a holistic approach, so perhaps a hand healer was not the leap in the dark it once was, although initially he had voiced one reservation.

'I wasn't too sure how the patients would accept the idea. But on the whole I've been very pleasantly surprised at the way they have accepted Lorraine. I don't pretend to understand everything, but a lot of her techniques are common sense and very sound – in particular the way she devotes a lot of time to the patient and then tailors any healing accordingly. In conventional medicine we're good at problem-solving but we're not always able to shape it to the individual. We have to accept that we cannot show how some alternative therapies work, and that conventional techniques are not always successful. So perhaps there's a place for these things to work in parallel.'

Dr Alastair Binnie has been in the practice for thirty years. 'Since Lorraine joined us I have discovered the enormous benefits she brings, not only to the patients, but also to ourselves. It is a giant move forward in terms of the practice, and has added another dimension to medicine. I discovered that the quackery I'd been told about as a student didn't apply. My teachers had no experience of this.'

But the future of psychic healing must be in the hands of younger doctors. Dr Simon Carruthers came to the practice in 1993. What are his views? 'When I first arrived here I gave no credence at all to the idea of "healing". But my experience over the last twelve months is that the transmission of healing energy to patients certainly seems to show a significant improvement of their symptoms. I'm increasingly becoming a believer in this form of treatment.'

GHOSTS AND POLTERGEISTS

It is said that everyone loves a good ghost story; perhaps because we enjoy being frightened by the unknown. It is also true that spectres and apparitions touch upon that timeless immortality of our soul. Britain is reputedly the most haunted nation on earth. From the spectral forms that haunt the oldest buildings to modern-day ghostly visitors unleashed amidst an urban sprawl; all of them suggest that there is more to life than we can possibly know. Then there are the poltergeists – violent, often unseen, rather interfering spirits that tend to wreak havoc on their unsuspecting victims. We have tried for centuries to fathom out such mysteries, seeking answers in fields as far apart as mental visions and other dimensions. This long hunt still continues, revealing fascinating new riddles along the way.

5
THE GHOSTS OF DOVER CASTLE

STEEPED in history and domestic intrigue, it is perhaps no wonder that so many castles are associated with ghost stories. Across Britain there are plenty with a reputation for being haunted. Standing on the ruined battlements of an ancient fortress, it is easy for present day visitors to conjure up the past. But are the ghosts more tangible than echoes of the past? Is there more at work than imagination? Do the dead really live on?

'HAUNTED' CASTLES – FACT OR FANTASY?

Accounts of haunted castles are hardly anything unusual. Stories abound of rattling chains, discarnate screams from the dungeons and apparitions of grey, white and black ladies.

Legends attach themselves to these sightings, as with the story of a butler who hanged himself at Glamis Castle (see below).

So the accounts seem to have tidy explanations. But what is the truth of these interpretations?

THE SECRETS OF GLAMIS CASTLE

Glamis Castle in Angus is famous for its ghosts and a grisly family secret. The castle's majestic fairytale towers (pictured on page 61) rise out of the wooded valley of Strathmore against a backdrop of the Grampian Mountains. Some of the present structure dates back to 1430. The castle was the childhood home of the Queen Mother, and her younger daughter, Princess Margaret, was born there.

Ghosts are thick on the ground at Glamis, which is a place of supernatural and human horror stories. There is the story of some members of the Ogilvy clan, who, fleeing from their enemies the Lindsays, sought protection at Glamis. The owner, Lord Strathmore, tricked them into entering a remote room. The door was then sealed and they were left to starve to death. Years later, another Lord Strathmore was disturbed by the sounds of bangings and anguished cries. He and some companions searched the castle until they located the room where the noises were coming from. When it was opened, Lord Strathmore is said to have collapsed.

Lord Crawford, an inveterate gambler, supposedly played dice with the Devil one night at Glamis, and died shortly afterwards. Several witnesses, including a daughter of Lord Castletown and the elder sister of the Queen Mother, Lady Granville, have seen his large bearded figure. The apparition is still seen even in the present day.

Further apparitions include a butler who hanged himself, a cruelly-treated servant boy, a tall dark man wearing a long coat buttoned to the neck, a figure in armour, a grey lady seen in the chapel and a white lady who was once seen independently by three witnesses. There is a terrifying figure of a tongueless woman seen looking out of a window – it is thought that her tongue was cut out to stop her gossiping about the family secret.

Such is the shame of this secret that no recent Earl has spoken of it to outsiders. The nature of the horror is only passed on to a Strathmore heir on his twenty-first birthday, and no female member of the family has been told. In the nineteenth century rumours abounded that Patrick, the third Earl, had fathered a deformed child, which in those less enlightened times was seen as a reflection of evil. This child was believed to have been locked away from prying eyes and to have lived to a great age. Evidence for this relies on the interpretation of an oil painting which now hangs in the drawing room of Glamis Castle. The picture shows the third Earl, seated, wearing a bronze breastplate. Standing to his right is the tall figure of a man. He too wears a breastplate, but it seems to fit a torso which is deformed. This impression is reinforced by a right arm which looks foreshortened.

Perhaps the truth of the family secret concerns not one deformed child but two or more.

The Castle is an archetypal symbol for supernatural manifestations. We *expect* them to be haunted. Castles feature heavily in the literature of horror. They are the turrets and dungeons where Count Dracula hangs out, places of

Glamis Castle, Angus, famous for its ghosts

unspeakable torture, trapdoors and secret passageways that lead to more horrors. And, as observers, commentators and story-tellers, we like neat endings and no loose strings. So the apparition seen where a butler hanged himself is identified as that man. There may not be any connection at all – but it gives the phenomenon an identity and makes a better story.

Investigations like the one carried out at Dover Castle demonstrate that, even when the layers are stripped away, there still remains an unidentifiable, inexplicable phenomenon that flouts the laws of 'rationalism'.

Ancient Dover Castle

Despite the large number of allegedly haunted castles in Britain, very few have produced both eye-witness reports and documentary evidence. When paranormal investigators decided to carry out a series of vigils at Dover in Kent, the castle's reputation was already well established.

Dover Castle overlooks the English Channel. Its ramparts are Iron Age, but the fortification was established by the Romans and the Anglo-Saxons; most of the present building is Norman, dating from the twelfth century. The labyrinth of tunnels beneath the castle were begun when Napoleon threatened to invade Britain, and extended at the beginning of the second world war. In 1940, men and equipment were moved in and the underground base became the nerve-centre for the Royal Navy's part in the evacuation of Dunkirk. These tunnels became known as Hellfire Corner.

Part of the labyrinth of tunnels beneath Dover Castle

So for many centuries the castle has been the focus for human activity, conducted at times under extreme emotional pressure. During the stress of war it could conceivably have become a sink hole, or battery, for human fears, hatred and death – the sort of place where some believe a 'psychical residue' of its former inhabitants might remain. Is it this 'residue' which has manifested regularly since the castle has been opened to the public as an exhibition centre?

In the castle grounds stands the restored church of St Mary-in-Castro, while a Roman lighthouse is situated at the west end. In the latter the ghosts of a Roman soldier and a hooded monk have been seen. The castle itself is said to be haunted by a drummer boy murdered during the Napoleonic Wars. Visitors have witnessed apparitions wearing the costume of the 1600s, principally a pikeman and a figure in Royalist garb.

MODERN GHOSTS

Tour guide Leslie Simpson vividly remembers an incident while showing a group of about twenty people around the Defence Telecommunications Repeater Station, situated in the underground tunnels of Hellfire Corner. He switched on a recorded commentary, and as it was ending he noticed that a woman was behaving rather oddly. 'She was looking very intently at something away from the group. Suddenly she got very alarmed and fell down, slipping on to her knee.'

Leslie went to help the woman and asked her if she had hurt herself. She said she was fine, but added: 'This is going to sound strange – but I think I should tell you what happened down there.'

She explained that she had been watching a man in naval uniform at the far end of the room. He was tinkering with some equipment, and she assumed he was one of the staff. Then he began walking towards the group of visitors. This alarmed her, because he was walking fast. As he reached the barrier he walked right through it and through her. At the moment of contact she spun around and, before losing her footing, saw him disappear through the exit. The woman convinced Leslie that she had experienced something.

Leslie subsequently took another group around the castle, but deliberately walked ahead of them while he first inspected the Repeater Station for the 'ghost'. There was nothing to be seen, but something else happened. In the room is a blue door leading to an annex. Usually it is closed, but on that occasion it was ajar – and something else was odd, too, Leslie noticed.

'There was a very strange noise coming from above. It was weird, a mechanical whining sound, intermixed with an animal noise. It frightened me, but as soon as I felt the fear the noise stopped. I've never heard that noise before nor since.'

*The Defence
Telcommunications
Repeater Station –
the most haunted
place in Hellfire
Corner*

A few months later an Italian tourist saw the same apparition near the equipment. He asked Leslie who the 'man' was, but neither the guide nor the other tourists could see anyone.

Another guide, Karen Mennie, also observed the odd reaction of a couple in the Repeater Station one summer's day in 1993. 'I noticed a father and daughter standing slightly away from the rest of the group. The girl appeared to be in communication with somebody who was invisible to me, and her father was looking on interestedly. All of a sudden the father disappeared out of the Repeater Station.' She went after the man and asked him to rejoin the others.

After her presentation she glibly told the group that the Defence Telecommunications Repeater Station was reputedly the most haunted place in the whole of Hellfire Corner. At this the father remarked: 'Yes, and I've just seen the ghost!'

Facing: *The Keep at Dover Castle*

Karen thought the man was just being funny, but afterwards he told her what had happened. Apparently he and his daughter had unknowingly been in conversation with a ghost. The father had then followed the figure out of the room. 'He was very casual about the whole thing,' said Karen, 'but the girl was very withdrawn and shaken. She looked in shock.'

The father told Karen what had been said. 'He said his name was Bill Billings, a Postal Telecommunications Officer from Canterbury, who had been killed whilst assembling one of the amplifier racks.'

Unfortunately, attempts to discover whether this man really existed, and was employed at the castle during the war, have met a brick wall. The records of military personnel based there during those years are not complete.

Clive Boreham of English Heritage, who own Dover Castle, says that inexplicable phenomena have been experienced by many others. For instance two Americans who visited the underground tunnels afterwards commented to the guides on the appropriate sound effects that had accompanied the tour. But there are no recorded effects down there.

Supernatural explanations

The Bill Billings case is not a typical one: in most recorded cases it appears that apparitions do not normally communicate with human observers. Most are described as seeming oblivious to anyone, giving rise to the theory that they are some sort of 'recording' left in the environment. Perhaps certain people who unknowingly have 'psychic' abilities are able to trigger off the recording, bringing the tableau to life for a few seconds.

But if there is recognition and communication between the two parties, then this cannot be the explanation. Perhaps, after all, apparitions are the surviving intelligences of once physical human beings, or supernatural entities masquerading as the same. When there is more than one witness, this must rule out hallucination as the answer.

SCEPTICAL ARGUMENTS

Not all the staff at Dover Castle are convinced that there is a supernatural explanation for these occurrences. Philip Wyborn-Brown has worked in the castle for eight years. He thinks the natural environment plays tricks on over-active imaginations. But he too has had an experience.

Facing: *Kenwood House, London, from where Vermeer's* **The Guitar Player** *was stolen (see Chapter 1)*

'We have a system here where we methodically search the buildings every evening to ensure that we don't lock anyone inside. I was locking up on one occasion, and I thought from the corner of my eye that I saw a figure pass the Great Hall and enter the King's Bed Chamber. I called to a colleague, but when we went into the room it was empty.

'The building is eight hundred years old, and creates its own sounds and shadows. It's built high on the cliff and is subject to a lot of wind and air currents. I think a lot of it is very much the natural phenomena of the building itself. I think the "figure" was a product of shadows.'

AN INVESTIGATION

Several overnight vigils have been carried out since 1991 by members of the local Thanet Psychic and Paranormal Research Unit and the Association for the Scientific Study of Anomalous Phenomena (ASSAP). Research co-ordinator Robin Laurence split the team of sixteen people into eight pairs, who were located at various points around the building. The vigil was conducted in four-hour shifts, and at the end of a shift each pair of observers would move to a different location. This ensured the investigators could not be responsible for phenomena. They brought with them sophisticated machines for sensing temperature changes and movements. Everyone was equipped with tape recorders, thermometers and still cameras; video cameras were also used.

On 12 October 1991 the team assembled at the castle, and at precisely 11.22 pm the first incident occurred. Investigator David Thomas was patrolling the passageway leading to the Spur, an arrowhead-shaped part of the fortification leading off from the Keep. Suddenly he heard a sound like a heavy wooden door slamming shut.

At 2.20 am two separate incidents were reported. Mary and Adrian Coombs-Hoar, positioned on the second floor of the Keep, heard a loud bang from behind locked doors leading to the west stairwell. Adrian unlocked the doors, but investigation revealed no rational cause for the noise and so he relocked them. As they walked away from them the wooden doors were suddenly shaken vigorously for a few seconds. Adrian said: 'We both jumped out of our skins, petrified, then went back to the door which was vibrating madly.'

Two members stationed in the lower St John's Tower area saw a shadowy figure moving slowly down the stone stairwell at the end of the Lower Caponier – a covered passage leading to the Spur. One of them called out to the figure, which turned and moved rapidly back up the stairs. They decided it must have been their colleague John Solley, but when they questioned him later he said he had not walked down the stairs at all during the shift – in fact,

---

**THINGS CLAIMED BY WITNESSES
OF HAUNTINGS**

- A sudden drop in temperature
- Inexplicable movement of objects
- Unaccountable knocks and bangs
- Fluctuations in the electro-magnetic field
- Malfunction of electrical equipment
- Subjective feeling that something is going to happen

---

at that precise moment he had been at the other end of the passageway leading to the Spur.

During the next shift these same two were to have a further experience. They were in the passageway formerly occupied by Solley when they twice heard a heavy wooden door being shut – at 3.30 am and 4.40 am. This was recorded on audio tape. Other members heard doors slamming in different parts of the castle, but the most significant event occurred at 5.20 am.

The second floor of the Keep, where the Coombs-Hoars had previously seen the double doors shaking, was the location for a second display of the phenomenon. This time the investigators were more prepared, and a video camera trained on the doors recorded the event. It had been placed there by Chris Cherry, a philosophy teacher from the University of Kent.

He and his companion were tired and drowsy at this point, but a sound similar to a key being turned in the door brought them round, just before the doors were once more vigorously shaken. A thorough and immediate check was made, but fraud was ruled out. The six seconds of film is very dramatic, as Cherry pointed out. 'The noise was quite tremendous, and all the tapestries above our heads started swaying. This was rather extraordinary. We thought we'd got a paranormal phenomenon and I very stupidly yelled out: ''We've got it!'' And that, of course, screwed the whole thing up.'

You can hear the investigator shout out on the film; the moment he does so the phenomenon stops. The door was shaking so violently that Chris Cherry doubts if any one person could have been responsible – and no one was missing from their post.

Investigator Ian Peters was walking up and down the base of St John's Tower when he was suddenly enveloped by an 'enormous sound'. 'It didn't frighten me so much as startle me out of my wits!' he said. 'Immediately afterwards there was a little ''ping'', as if someone had dropped a pebble on the nearby wooden stairs. Afterwards we experimented, but couldn't duplicate the effect.' There were three other witnesses to the sound.

A photograph taken from the six-second film of the rattling doors

During the second vigil, on 30 November 1991, a tape recorder was discovered switched off in the Mural Gallery of the Keep, and later the sound of it being interfered with was recorded. In this same location a strong smell of perfume was detected by the team, and in the basement area of the Keep two loud thuds were heard.

TUNING IN

It is not unusual for investigators to introduce a psychic into a haunted building. Psychics claim to be able to tune into the world of the Unseen and pick up information and emotions left by the dead. This was done during the filming of *Strange But True?* at Dover Castle, with mixed results.

Michael Bromley is a burly six-footer, bearded, with shoulder length hair, who claims to commune with the spirit world. He spent seven years in

America working with Native Indians, searching for missing persons and even sniffing out security loopholes as official psychic to the Los Angeles Olympic Games.

Would Michael pick anything up at Dover Castle? It was a disappointing night. Most of what he said had little relevance. He came up with a name, 'Helen', but it meant nothing at the time.

A few days later the *Strange But True?* office received a telephone call from the castle. An Australian tourist who could not have known about the filming visited the castle and described seeing a man's ghost. Was this the mysterious 'Bill Billings'? The apparition was very agitated. He kept repeating a name. *Helen.*

The staff at Dover Castle, normally blase to such stories, were stunned by this one. As Clive Boreham of English Heritage said: 'You could have knocked me down with a feather. It was amazing really. It sort of changed my attitude to the place.'

6

HIGHWAY
OF HORROR?

WHEN we make major changes to the natural environment, do we run the risk of disrupting something more than the habitats of wildlife, or a landscape of trees and rocks? Is it possible that such changes affect not only our world, but also other, invisible dimensions that occasionally impinge on ours? When the earth-movers drove a road through the ancient crags above the small Yorkshire town of Stocksbridge, what else did they disturb?

Some fringe science researchers believe that the earth is crisscrossed with electromagnetic lines called leys. They suggest that when these are disrupted negative phenomena occur, such as paranormal effects and accident black spots. Is it pseudo-scientific mumbo-jumbo, or an explanation for the events around Stocksbridge?

Ghost stories make good entertainment, but there is a serious side too. To the percipient – the person at the centre of the experience – they are often very frightening. In some cases the fear can be so extreme that it has a long-term negative effect, as happened at Stocksbridge.

The calibre of a haunting is enhanced by the number of independent witnesses and their reputations for reliability. The percipients of Stocksbridge included two security guards and two police officers. Such people are trained observers used to working at night and to the tricks played by light and the natural environment. They are not the sort to be taken in by their imagination – are they?

The lie of the land

Stocksbridge lies across a valley in South Yorkshire, surrounded by steep escarpments 2,000 feet above sea level and a huddle of villages. This is rugged moorland country, broken only by reservoirs and the occasional pine forest. Despite modern roads, it gets cut off every winter whenever there is heavy snow.

70

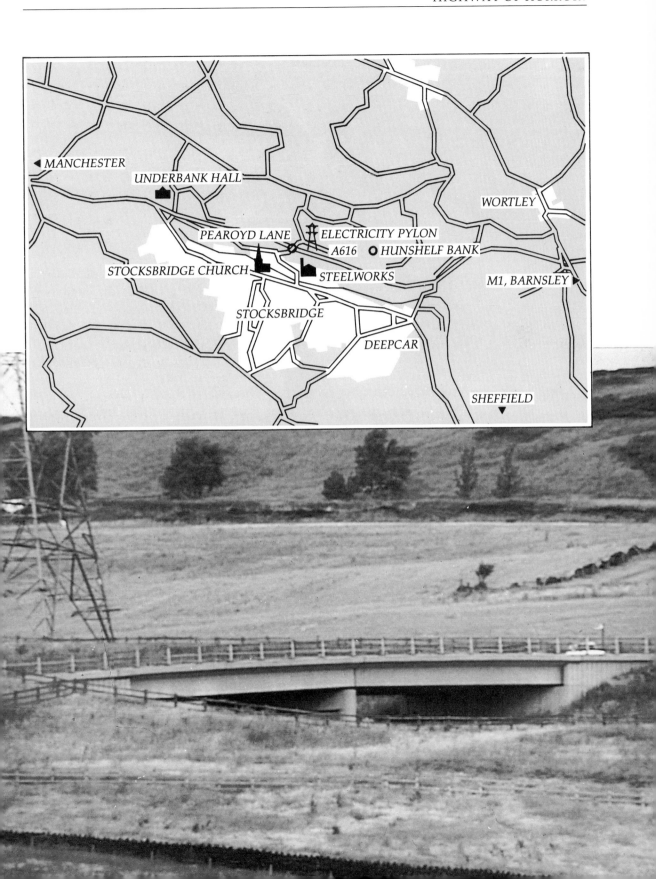

MANCHESTER

UNDERBANK HALL

WORTLEY

PEAROYD LANE

ELECTRICITY PYLON

A616   HUNSHELF BANK

STOCKSBRIDGE CHURCH

STEELWORKS

M1, BARNSLEY

STOCKSBRIDGE

DEEPCAR

SHEFFIELD

The town is seven miles north of Sheffield on the A616. Trouble apparently started when highway planners decided to build a by-pass around the town, and to link the A628 Barnsley to Manchester road over the Pennines with the M1.

Most of the phenomena were located along a stretch of road carved into the steep hillside above the steelworks at Stocksbridge. At this point it cut through Pearoyd Lane, which winds over the moors before dropping down into the town. The lane was disrupted because of the building work, and impassable. A bridge was being constructed which would reconnect Pearoyd Lane, but at this stage only the middle pillars and lintel were finished; it was still an island, only accessible via long ladders, in the huge trench gouged out of the earth.

In September 1987 the £14 million bypass was in the final stages of completion when the strange events began.

Insecurity

Close to midnight on 7 September, two security men, Steven Brookes and David Goldthorpe, were going about their normal routine. They were employed by Constant Security Services and had been guarding the Stocksbridge building site for a couple of months, often working at night.

Strange Figures

Alongside the uncompleted road stood an electricity pylon. As the men drove past they came across a bewildering sight. Beneath the giant struts a group of four or five children wearing 'old-fashioned clothes' were dancing in a circle. The men stopped the vehicle and climbed out, but the 'children' had vanished. There were not even any footprints in the fresh mud beneath the pylon.

They continued their patrol, then headed back. As they neared the bridge, they saw a strange white-hooded figure perched on it. The guards knew there was no easy way for anyone to have climbed up there. They drove off the road up a ramp and stopped on Pearoyd Lane in line with the bridge. The hooded figure was still on the parapet. David Goldthorpe put the car headlights on main beam, and the light passed right through the figure. Then it was gone!

Brookes and Goldthorpe were so unnerved that they finished their shift early and drove over to Constant Security's headquarters at nearby Mexborough. They called out their boss, Peter Owens.

'When I arrived, the guards were in a very distressed condition. They had cups of tea but their hands were shaking as they tried to drink. The men were

pallid and very much in shock. One of the guards was actually crying.' It took one and a half hours to obtain a coherent story from the men. 'I've been in the security industry a long time and have heard a lot of things. They'd definitely seen something. It was very difficult to disbelieve them. They were convincing and stuck to their story. Both guards had been with us a number of years and were very experienced. I wouldn't say they were easily frightened, but were used to working at remote sites.'

An artist's impression of the 'children' seen dancing beneath the electricity pylon

HELP FROM THE POLICE

Managing director Michael Lee, a former policeman, telephoned the police and told PC Dick Ellis: 'They've worked for me for a number of years – they're good lads and they've seen something.'

The constable was naturally sceptical, but his own experience was to change all that dramatically. Brookes and Goldthorpe went across to

Deepcar police station. PC Dick Ellis remembers it well. 'The security guards were known to me. They appeared very nervous and agitated, and said they weren't going back on site until something had been done. It was obvious they were spooked, but I said it wasn't really a police matter, and perhaps they needed help from the Church.'

The men took Ellis at his word. They went to the local church and refused to leave until the bypass had been exorcised. PC Ellis went up to the church and eventually the men agreed to go. The officer took them more seriously now, and decided to do some research.

'I spoke to local historians, visited the library and talked to old folk. I did discover a story several centuries old about a monk who had left a local monastery and gone to live at Underbank Hall, which is at the end of the bypass. One day he left the hall to visit Stocksbridge market. The weather was very bad and he completely vanished.

'I also turned up a story dating back 150 years. Several children were travelling down Hunshelf Bank in a cart in the area of the bypass, when it turned over, killing them all. But there is no official documentation for this – it's more folklore.'

Paranormal researchers David Clarke and Ralph Knutt, who initially investigated the case, discovered that workmen living near the site had heard children's voices in the middle of the night, and a recluse living on the hillside also reported seeing 'children' dancing under a pylon and around a caravan.

On 12 September PC Ellis and Special Constable John Beet went up to the location around midnight. PC Ellis had purposely kept his intentions quiet.

'I'd decided I was going up there to see if I could turn anything up. This was mainly out of curiosity, not because I believed in ghosts. I was out in the Panda car with John. I hadn't told any of my other colleagues because they would have set me up. Even John didn't know until a couple of hours earlier. He was game for it, so we went on to the bypass from the Deepcar end.'

It was deserted up there. The two security guards had refused to resume their duties and had not been replaced.

'It was little more than a dirt track then,' PC Ellis continued, 'and we parked roughly halfway between the pylon and the bridge where the two sightings had supposedly been. We turned all the lights and radios off. It was a clear sky, virtually a full moon, and after a while we could see clearly. If anyone came near us we could see him.'

They were directly above the steelworks, which added light to the moonlit landscape with an eerie orange glow from its furnaces. On the bridge was a white painted pallet box, and after a few minutes Ellis asked Beet if he could see anything amiss.

'We could see a shadow, so I put the full beam on the car and saw nothing at all. After our eyes had adjusted, we drove up and got out – not a damned thing! We drove back to where we were before, and lo and behold, there was something moving around the box...'

They went up again. This time, unlike the week before, there was a ladder leaning against the bridge. PC Ellis climbed up it and found some polythene flapping around in the breeze. He secured it with bricks and returned to the car.

'We decided that this was causing the movement, or the lights from the steelworks were reflecting off the box and creating shadows. Back at our original spot I put my window down. It was a nice night. I was in the driver's seat, John was in the passenger seat.'

Amused at how they had been 'spooked', the officers decided to wait another ten or fifteen minutes, then resume their normal patrol.

FROZEN WITH FEAR

'Suddenly I had a feeling, unlike any I'd had before, just as if someone had walked over my grave, because I froze. And what was so odd, I went cold without knowing why. It was a feeling of total helplessness, like I was paralysed. I couldn't move my arms, I couldn't move my legs, I couldn't speak.

'A few seconds after, I had another feeling that someone was stood at the side of me. I managed to cast my head to the right, and saw something by the side of the car.'

PC Ellis was staring at the upper torso of a figure wearing light clothing with a 'V' on the chest. Suddenly it was gone and instantaneously reappeared around the passenger side of the vehicle. Special Constable John Beet let out a scream and hit his colleague on the arm. He got a more detailed look at the figure.

'To me, what I saw of him, it sort of connected to the 1800s – that kind of era. It had a wizened face and pointed nose, and it was staring with piercing eyes. I looked again and tried to focus, and it was gone...'

Beet also felt very cold and unable to move. 'My main aim then was to get out, to go, get off the bypass!'

PC Ellis leaped out of the car and desperately looked around, even under the vehicle. There was no time for anyone to have run away. But there was no sign of anyone either, and the only footprints were their own.

He climbed back in and drove up to Pearoyd Lane, parking where the security guards had stopped the week before. PC Ellis radioed for other officers to join them. As they waited, a terrific bang suddenly sounded from the rear of the car.

'We thought someone had run into the back of the vehicle,' PC Ellis said, 'or hit it. But there wasn't a jolt – the car didn't move at all.'

The officers jumped out, and as they did so a series of bangs sounded. PC Ellis likened it to someone hitting the car with a baseball bat or a pickaxe handle. 'It was clearly an attack upon the vehicle,' he added.

They drove away as fast as they could, and met their colleagues part way up the hillside. As Ellis and Beet told them what had happened, the other officers were not slow in making fun of their story.

Back at the station the sergeant could see that they were genuinely frightened. A search was made of the bypass, but with no result, and a careful examination of the Panda car revealed not even a scratch.

A never-ending story

The bypass opened early in 1988 – on Friday the thirteenth! So perhaps it is no surprise that the phenomena continued.

David and Judi Simpson were returning home after visiting a relative one Friday evening at the end of July 1992. They were driving towards Wortley, across the top of the bypass, when they were confronted by an amazing sight.

In a field to their left was a grey figure 'jogging'. It had a head, arms and legs, but no facial characteristics. Mrs Simpson commented: 'It was actually running above ground level towards the edge of the field. The arm movements were not co-ordinated with the legs at all. It was a totally erratic mess. As it reached the embankment near the road, it kind of rose up and disappeared right in front of the car.'

Mrs Simpson braked automatically, although there was no sensation of a collision. 'There was a feeling of total disbelief. I've never experienced anything like that before.'

David Simpson added: 'I felt quite scared. A chill ran down my back and goose bumps came up on my arms. It was a shock!'

In a previous incident, in the autumn of 1987, Graham Brooke and his son Nigel were jogging near Wortley at dusk when they saw an apparition. Graham was training for the London Marathon and was ahead of his son. He looked over his shoulder for Nigel and when he faced forward again there was a figure walking up the middle of the road towards him. Graham thought it was a dangerous occupation and decided to wait in a lay-by, watching as the figure drew nearer.

'My eyes were telling me one thing and my brain another. The chap wasn't normal. He was wearing a brown cape which was buttoned down the front, and gaiters. The clothing looked seventeenth-century. As he got nearer I could see he had a black face and no eyes...'

By this time Nigel had joined his father. He confirmed that the face was featureless, lacking a nose and mouth. Both witnesses noticed that the figure was walking below the current level of the road. 'It seemed to be dragging a bag, but of course the bottom half was not visible because it was below the road surface.'

The two described how the hairs stood up on the back of their necks. As the figure passed by, both noticed a very peculiar smell, 'a dusty smell, like old newspapers,' Nigel said. Graham described it as 'fusty, like an antique shop'.

Feeling afraid, they started jogging again – in the opposite direction to the figure. Suddenly, the apparition vanished.

Psychic contact

In these situations local psychics inevitably become involved. Supposedly, their enhanced awareness of the 'spirit world' allows them to make contact with supernatural entities. Would they be able to throw light on the Stocksbridge haunting?

When psychic Elisa Wilkinson heard about the hauntings she decided to investigate. Accompanied by her daughter Lesley, she drove to the location and parked in the same place as the police officers had done. It was 11pm. The bridge now linked both sides of Pearoyd Lane, although traffic was restricted to single file. Temporary traffic lights were operating at either end. The women sat there for a while, then Elisa decided they should leave the car.

'As soon as I said, "Let's go and look around", the traffic lights began to go berserk!'

PUSHED BY AN UNSEEN FORCE

They climbed out, put their boots on and locked up. As they walked in the direction of the bridge, Mrs Wilkinson realised she had left her gloves behind, and went back.

'I was only a few feet away from the car when the back door opened on its own. The gloves were on the seat.'

She put them on and returned to her daughter. The two began climbing up the steep embankment to Pearoyd Lane; their feet made a crunching noise on the freezing, muddy slope. Part way up, they heard footsteps coming from behind. They stopped and swung round. They were carrying torches, but could see no one. The footsteps continued.

'They came right up to us, and stopped. Then we were pushed. Lesley first, and then me. We were pushed until we couldn't go any further. We were right under the bridge at this point, with a steep drop on the other side. I told her not to be afraid. When I tried to move away, I was pushed back again.'

As they tried to take stock of the situation and stay calm, it suddenly started to become very warm. It grew so hot that they loosened their coats and took their scarves and gloves off.

'Feel where the heat ends and the cold begins,' she instructed Lesley. They stretched out their arms and discovered they were in an eight-foot diameter circle of heat. The temperature became unbearable but this time, when they tried to move, it was unhindered. The pair went back down to the car and discovered it was 3am. They had lost over three hours.

A STENCH OF DECAYING FLESH

Elisa sat in the car trying to communicate with the 'presence', but without success. 'It was blocking me out. As a rule I can communicate with the spirit people, but not with this one.' It was so cold outside that the car was steamed up, so they wound the windows down.

'A terrible smell came into the car – it was like decaying flesh. Then a figure appeared on Lesley's side. Our legs started to go numb. I successfully fought against it, but Lesley became paralysed. The figure was completely black, cloaked, and it had a hood. There was a bad feeling about it, evil. It walked – or rather floated – across the bonnet to my side, then around the boot and back to Lesley, where it disappeared.'

As soon as it was gone, the paralysis lifted. Mrs Wilkinson wondered if

LOST TIME

People who claim to have experienced anomalous events sometimes report a period they cannot account for. This seems to occur more often during UFO encounters, but also manifests in other types of exeriences too. What is the cause of this amnesia? There are two possible explanations.

Part of the encounter is so horrific that the subconscious has blanked it out from the conscious mind. This is common with victims of serious accidents or physical attack, and is a natural protective measure of the mind.

This explanation becomes less tenable when groups of witnesses experience the same period of missing time. People vary in their threshold of handling terror. Some would remember the whole experience, others would suffer different amounts of amnesia.

Experients seem to be in an altered state of consciousness during encounters. Is this a subjective psychological phenomenon, or is it 'mind control' by an outside source? In this scenario amnesia would have been purposely created by an 'intelligence'. There are certain things it, or they, would not want victims to remember.

Some do 'remember', however. Missing time can return months or years later in flashbacks and nightmares. Hypnotic regression seems to be a short cut to this natural leaching through of supposed repressed memories. But are these 'memories' genuine or fantasy?

someone was playing games. She did what PC Ellis had done – climbed out of the car and looked around. Like PC Ellis, she found no one.

Lesley was very afraid now, so they drove home.

A grim reaper

Lucinda June, a psychic from nearby Penistone, became convinced that sightings of the hooded figure were proof that the road had disturbed the spirit of a monk.

The psychic claimed that while travelling on the road she felt a presence in the seat next to her.

'Just as I went through the cutting where they blasted all the rocks I became intensely cold. A strong smell came into the car like old musty books. It got stronger, and I felt something like hands pushing into my back. Then a solid blackness formed in the passenger seat.

Underbank Hall where a Cistercian monk, disillusioned with monastic life, was believed to have found employment

'There was no discernible figure, but it was so dense I couldn't see through it. I became very frightened and started saying the Lord's Prayer, but it was still there. I started to feel as though I could not move. I'm not usually scared of the psychic world, but my stomach went very tight.'

Suddenly, it was gone. The following day, when she was calmer, Lucinda went back and communicated with the spirit of a monk. It had been killed in tragic circumstances, although no details were forthcoming.

'Something very bad must have happened to this spirit. It's stuck in time. I've actually called it the Grim Reaper because of the intense feeling of sadness it brings with it.'

DEATH ON THE ROAD

In the first five years after the bypass opened, there were many serious accidents and eight deaths. Sheffield Hillsborough MP Helen Jackson called for the bypass to be officially declared an 'accident black spot'. The accidents were blamed on design faults but Lucinda June believes the accidents are caused by the ghost. Only time will tell.

The historical facts

Trevor Lodge is a local historian who is often asked about the rumours that the spirit of a monk is haunting the Stocksbridge bypass.

'The belief is that the hooded figure that has been seen is that of a monk, and there is strong evidence that monks worked in this valley in the twelfth century. They were granted land rights and privileges by Norman knights who came over with William the Conqueror. The knights did this in the belief that they would obtain eternal salvation.

'The monks followed agricultural pursuits, but it is said that one of them, a Cistercian, grew disillusioned with their autocratic way of life and found employment in Underbank Hall. When he died he was buried in unconsecrated ground which was disturbed by the bypass.'

Is there any reason why children should be haunting the bypass?

'The most likely explanation is that these children are associated in some way with mining, which was quite widespread in the valley from about the 1760s. We know that the coal mines here were operated with children as part of the labour force. In fact there was a colliery called Hunshelf Pit immediately on the hillside below Pearoyd Lane, near the bypass. The only problem is that we don't have any records of a mining accident involving children, and they were well documented from the mid-1830s.'

Inquest

The Stocksbridge case presents two separate issues. Did the witnesses experience objective paranormal events and, if they did, was the source the surviving personalities of the dead?

Astonishingly, most of the Stocksbridge 'ghost' sightings involved multiple witnesses. Usually apparitions are observed by people on their own, encouraging the belief that the phenomenon represents a complex subjective process involving hallucinations. These shared experiences quash that idea.

The sets of witnesses all agree on what took place. Given the weight and quality of eye-witness reports, is it reasonable to believe that something objective, and paranormal, broke out in earnest at about the time the bypass was under construction?

Human nature being what it is, people are not content with accepting the conclusion that a paranormal phenomenon was manifesting to witnesses; they have to weave a story around it. There were 'children' dancing around the struts of an electricity pylon, so they must be the spirits of youngsters killed in an accident. Some witnesses describe a hooded figure, so that becomes the trapped spirit of a monk. Cue local legends and folklore to complete this story.

But these experiences are more complex than that, and this may not do them justice.

ILL EFFECTS

Whatever the true source of the phenomenon, one thing is certain – the absolute terror that it can generate in some of its victims. Steven Brookes and David Goldthorpe, the security guards who brought the events to everyone's attention, paid dearly for their encounter with the Unknown. One left his job three days later, and the other would only remain providing he worked regular days – but not on the Stocksbridge bypass. Even so, he too resigned after several months.

Even the most hardened cynic must admit that *something* extremely odd has been happening in Stocksbridge. The power of imagination must not be underestimated but does there come a time where a paranormal explanation fits the facts better?

7
PETE THE POLTERGEIST

THE word poltergeist is German for 'noisy spirit'. And wherever they are reported, they certainly seem to cause a stir. Unlike most ghosts, poltergeists react to their surroundings – and their victims. Sometimes their actions can be sinister, but more often than not they are mischievous, playing childish tricks like emptying sugar from a jar or drawing on a wall.

That such forces manifest themselves is well-documented. But what are they?

A believer will cite the disappearance of small objects as evidence of supernatural intervention. A sceptic will argue it is all down to absent-mindedness. How many of us have found things gone from where we left them, only to turn up somewhere else?

When investigators appear, poltergeists usually disappear. But the case of Pete the Poltergeist, investigated by the Society for Psychic Research (SPR), turned out to be one of the longest-running poltergeist cases ever recorded. It went on for five years.

'SIGNS' OF A POLTERGEIST

- The sighting of an apparition
- Non-human noises
- Footsteps
- Scraping sounds
- The manifestation of foreign objects
- Levitations
- The disappearance of small items
- Spontaneous combustion
- 'Vandalism' of furnishings
- Potentially violent acts
- Spontaneous writing

A well-documented case

David Fontana, a university psychology professor, began to investigate the case for the SPR after it came to the Society's notice in 1989. The result was a detailed paper called 'A Responsive Poltergeist: A Case from South Wales'.

This photograph shows the vandalism reputedly caused by a poltergeist in the home of Ken Webster in Dodleston, Chester (May 1985)

The case revolved around a small business in Cardiff called Mower Services and the adjoining retail shop. Started in the late 1970s by John and Pat Matthews and Pat's brother Fred Cook, the business repaired and sold lawn mowers. John, Pat and Fred, their relatives and employees, together with customers and business callers all claimed to have experienced the phenomenon.

It started with stones bouncing off the roof. Naturally the owners thought that children were responsible, and on several occasions John ran outside – but there was never anyone in sight. Stones hit the windows, too, and on at least six occasions the police were called. But the phenomenon was about to move indoors. When it did, things began to happen in earnest.

Small objects such as stones, coins and bolts were seen flying across the workshop: they impacted on the walls and occasionally hit someone, but without hurting them. At first the group suspected that one of them was playing a joke, but as the incidents continued this interpretation became increasingly less likely. A paint scraper went missing and suddenly reappeared, hot to the touch, as if it had been heated with a blowlamp. In the business premises upstairs a diary disappeared from a drawer and turned up on the roof of a nearby building. There were frequent telephone calls to John and Pat's house at all hours, sometimes every few minutes, but there was never anyone on the line. Telephone engineers could find nothing wrong.

Many of the incidents were childish. For instance a bunch of keys went missing, and while everyone was searching for them they came shooting across the floor.

THE RESPONSIVE POLTERGEIST

To deal with the suspicion that one of them might be responsible for staging a hoax, the staff decided on a test. They locked up the premises and then stood around a bench, each of them placing their hands in plain view of the others. There was no one in the building but them.

'Throw us a stone,' John requested.

They were amazed when a stone fell on to the table.

Then one of them said: 'Hang on, if we are doing this as a proper test, we should be writing it down.'

Obligingly, a pen dropped on to the floor, followed by a sheet of headed notepaper which had originated in the office on the floor above. They asked for a spark plug, and one instantly dropped on the table. When Fred asked for a sovereign, a Jubilee coin dropped from the air. This belonged to John, and was usually kept in a drawer at home!

'We were there for two hours,' John said. 'I went home and told my wife I'd just spent the most fascinating hours of my life.'

From then on the mysterious source of the phenomena was endowed with a personality. The family nicknamed it Pete ... Pete the Poltergeist. It was at this point that they called in Professor David Fontana.

ENTER THE PROFESSOR

'I made my first visit to the premises on the afternoon of Wednesday, 28 June. I came along the private alleyway at the side and entered the yard at the back of the workshop through the open door. Simultaneously with my entrance, there was a loud "ping" as if a missile had struck machinery. John, who was sitting nearby talking to a sales representative, his hands in full view, looked up at me and remarked without surprise: "There you are, he's greeting you!"'

The projectile was a small stone. Professor Fontana was impressed for two reasons: first, because clearly neither of the two men in the yard was involved, and second, because it is rare for an investigator to be present when poltergeist activity is actually taking place. As a result he was prepared to take this case very seriously.

On subsequent visits Professor Fontana claimed to witness further phenomena. He was lightly struck by a stone and a ball bearing, observed a coin disappear and reappear, saw a heavy magnifying glass hit the floor violently, and observed a pen which appeared when 'Pete' was asked to bring one.

One of the hallmarks of the poltergeist is its *potential* for causing injury. On one occasion Pat had a narrow escape. She had entered the workshop from the retail shop by an adjoining door and just as she was closing the door behind her, a large steel strimming wheel crashed against it. As Professor Fontana, who witnessed the incident, pointed out: 'Had the object arrived a split second sooner it would in all probability have struck her a serious blow on the back of the head.'

Several times a brass case from an old 25lb wartime shell that happened to be in the room was thrown violently across it. Fearing for the safety of staff and visitors, John removed it to the yard outside. While he was working at his bench, the case crashed down beside him. When Pete was ordered to 'fire the shell', blue flames came from it.

The phenomena escalated. A number of times they discovered that the table in the small kitchen at the back of the premises had been crudely laid with cutlery and cups. At the end of one day which had been particularly active John remarked to Pat: 'We've had everything except wood.' With that he described how a plank of wood came hurtling into the shop and took a chunk out of the adjoining door.

*John and
Pat Matthews,
owners of the
haunted Mower
Services in Cardiff*

Joyce Glenn was one of the many customers who also witnessed things. 'I was just as sceptical as everybody else. I heard about this poltergeist, and was in the shop one day when little nuts and bolts were flying around and dropping from nowhere. It was incredible and quite scary!' Another customer was in the shop when he was suddenly showered with manure. He left hurriedly without waiting for his change!

One night thieves broke into Mower Services, forcing the front door and stealing £1,200 worth of stock. When Gareth Lucas came to make an assessment for the insurance claim, he observed more than he had bargained for. 'I saw and heard stones being thrown around and being thrown on the floor. There were two men there but they certainly weren't throwing the stones. When I asked them what it was about, I was told: 'Oh, that's Pete the Poltergeist''.' When Gareth filed his assessment, mentioning the poltergeist, he suffered quite a bit of ribbing in the office. Until, that is, his colleague Reg Jenkin – making the excuse of a fire risk survey – went to Mower Services, and he too was amazed by what was happening with the stones.

At a later stage in the haunting, Pete even left money. On opening the premises each morning the staff would find a £5 or £10 note stuck to the ceiling tiles. Fred even claims he found one pasted to the wet windscreen of his car. Altogether, apparently, they collected £70!

PETE ON THE PROWL

The intrusion into the homes of the business partners was more extensive than anonymous telephone calls. Once, five £1 coins violently struck Fred's front door as he was crossing the darkened hallway. Carburettor floats, used to control the flow of petrol inside the lawn mower engines and stored at the workshop, were often found stuck into ceilings. Fred was sometimes 'attacked' by the needle end of a carburettor. On one occasion he, his wife and sister were sitting under a parasol in the garden when they saw a carburettor needle being pushed through the material from above.

Others were affected by Pete, too. Christine Windels observed something bizarre in her nearby charity shop: 'The most amazing thing was this piece of string coming through the ceiling. It came through, curled back on itself into a knot, came through a little bit more, curled back on itself and then dropped to the floor. I looked at the ceiling but there were no holes, nothing at all!'

A Baptist church next to Mower Services also experienced poltergeist phenomena, as the Revd Mike Fuller attested. 'One evening I was working up here in the office and stones started hitting the window. I did everything I

Wales on Sunday featured the story in July 1991

could to find out what it was. There were no people down there. I went down and looked around, but there was nobody that could be throwing stones. I came back upstairs and the whole business continued.' Mike and several other church members went out and prayed around the boundary of the premises. After that, they claim, the phenomenon stopped.

PETE IN PERSON?

During 1991 Fred Cook saw an apparition. On opening the workshop door he describes being confronted by the sight of a small boy sitting on a shelf near the ceiling. He was wearing short trousers and a peaked cap, but there was no face beneath the cap, and no knees. Fred called out: 'Hello! What are you doing here?' as if he was speaking to a real boy. In reply, a carburettor float was thrown at him. Then the apparition vanished.

On the second occasion, Fred and John were working on a mower in the middle of the workshop. Again, Fred caught sight of the small boy sitting on the shelf. Slowly, he told John to turn around and look, but before he could, half a house brick came hurtling down and hit the mower.

Then one morning Fred saw Pete sitting on the counter beside the till, swinging his legs. As he walked towards the apparition it faded into nothing. Later, Fred was locking up the premises and walking towards the rear exit. Suddenly, he saw the small figure standing silhouetted in the light from the open washroom door. The figure seemed to be waving goodbye. This, which was to be the last direct sighting, deeply disturbed Fred. He tried to describe the figure. 'A little boy in 1940s' clothes, boots up to his ankles, little cub cap on his head. He had a little short coat. You could imagine he was all grey, no face – but the face was *there*. It's hard to explain. All you could see was his hand waving.'

In 1933, when Mower Services outgrew its old premises and moved to a new industrial estate in Cardiff, the only activity which continued was in Fred's home.

'We had little pictures turn in their frames ... spoons being thrown upstairs ... we had a little blue jug that disappeared. Four days later, it came back. We decided to break the jug when we moved home because we didn't want it to follow us.'

To date, Fred Cook has seen no more of Pete the Poltergeist.

The Professor's report

Sceptics cite the activities of small animals such as mice, underground streams, vibrations from machinery and passing traffic, lapses of memory,

*The apparition of a
small boy was seen
in the workshop*

tricks of perception and fraud as the explanations for 'poltergeist' phenomena. Certainly all these causes could be, and have been, successfully applied
to some cases as a partial or full explanation. Professor David Fontana, who
as the man on the spot is more qualified than most to give an informed
opinion, applied these options to the Cardiff events.

In his reports to the Society for Psychical Research, he made the following
observations. The possible activities of animals such as mice or cats could
only be applied to one incident. There was no reason to suggest that exterior
vibrations played any part at all. While it was conceded that lapses of
memory might explain a few instances where objects had 'disappeared',
they played no part in the deluge of other events.

Fraud is always a possibility in such cases, but Fontana professed to find
all the witnesses to be consistent and reliable persons who had nothing
to gain. There was nothing to cast a shadow over them. The activity went
on over a five-year period – too long for a practical joke by person or
persons unknown. Indeed, the professor knew from personal experience
that it would have been impossible for fraud to have taken place. During
one of his experiments David Fontana would throw a stone into a
corner, and Pete would then throw it back. He discovered 'active corners'
of the premises from which Pete would return anything thrown into
them.

The professor did consider whether Fred Cook's perception was playing tricks with regard to the appearance of the apparition, but he decided against it for a number of reasons. While the light conditions on every occasion were poor, the apparition had the same appearance each time. On the first two instances, the sightings were accompanied with projectiles – also witnessed once by John Matthews.

It might be suggested that Fred had 'conjured up' the image of a small boy. Much of the phenomena was reminiscent of schoolboy pranks, and there was a rumour that a small boy had been killed in the back yard at some unspecified time. As John Matthews commented: 'As time went by I could sense that this thing wanted to play, like a child. I would be there in the evening checking the till and would see little things flying across the room. I would ignore it and carry on with my work, and then later it would come near and hit me on the leg. Then I would put a few things out for it to play with, and go back to work. Five or ten minutes later I would go back and everything would be disturbed.'

But a schoolboy was the last thing on Fred Cook's mind. He had already discussed the possibility that his own deceased father might be behind the activity, an idea that occurred to him when some coins bearing his father's year of birth appeared. So if the apparition *was* a trick of the mind, surely Fred would have created an image of his own father?

OTHER FAMOUS POLTERGEIST CASES

Sauchie in Scotland was the location for manifestations surrounding eleven-year-old Virginia Campbell during November and December 1960. A particular feature of this haunting was said to be the levitation of objects, which was witnessed by both the local vicar and the family doctor. The case was investigated by Professor A. R. G. Owen, lecturer in mathematics and genetics at Cambridge University. Margaret Stewart, Virginia's school-teacher, was interviewed by paranormal investigator Malcolm Robinson in 1993. Ms Stewart confirmed several events that she had witnessed in school, including one occasion when Virginia's desk had risen four feet above the floor!

The Rosenheim poltergeist – named after a firm of lawyers near Munich, whose offices the entity haunted – concentrated on effects of an electrical nature. During 1967 and 1968 light bulbs exploded, fuses blew and the telephone system went berserk, recording dozens of calls which had never been made. Electricians and telephone engineers were called into the offices, but no matter what they did, the disturbances continued.

In desperation the lawyers invited parapsychologist Professor Hans Bender to try and solve the mystery. After investigating the circumstances he realised that the phenomena revolved around one of the employees, a nineteen-year-old clerk called Annemarie. Indeed, as she walked past light fittings they began to swing. Annemarie eventually left her job, and the disturbances stopped.

There was havoc in a council house in Enfield, North London, during 1977. It involved four children and their mother, and the phenomena began when the beds of two of the children began to shake. The following night the sound of someone shuffling across the carpet was heard. Loud knocks followed, and a chest of drawers was seen to move. When a neighbour searched the house more knocks were heard and the police were called out, but they could do nothing.

Maurice Grosse was called in to investigate the mysterious happenings in Enfield, North London. One of the children was apparently hurled out of bed by the poltergeist

Then objects were thrown around the house, including Lego bricks and marbles; one of the marbles was found to be hot. Paranormal experts Maurice Grosse and Guy Lyon Playfair became involved in investigations for the Society of Psychical Research. The phenomena intensified and some were captured on film by a national newspaper photographer. A gas fire was ripped off a wall, apparitions were seen and then a strange voice was heard, claiming it was 'Joe Watson'. Altogether the investigators recorded over four hundred incidents. Some members of the SPR thought that the girls might be involved in a fraud, but the investigators disagreed. The phenomena ceased at the end of 1978.

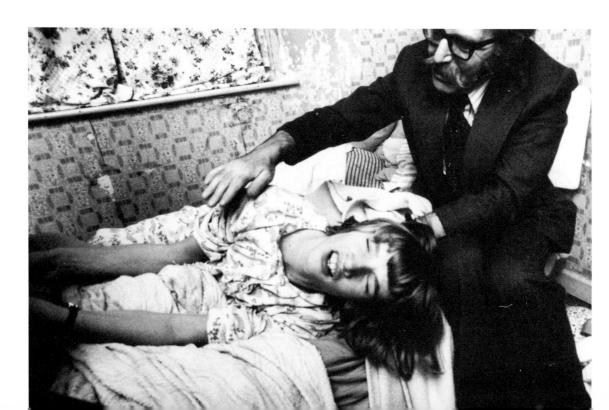

WHAT, THEN, IS A 'POLTERGEIST'?

Maurice Grosse comments: 'There are two main theories regarding poltergeist activity. The first is that the mental attitude of people can affect their physical surroundings, move things around and cause other things to occur like apparitions, pools of water and fire. In the second theory proponents believe that the phenomena are caused by outside entities. I know these things happen because I have experienced so much of it myself.'

Parapsychologists believe that poltergeist phenomena are the result of repressed emotional trauma, usually experienced by adolescents such as those involved in the Sauchie and Enfield cases. This mental energy is then exteriorised and starts playing havoc with the environment. They frequently cite young girls as being the cause of this activity. But this analysis is flawed on several counts.

The Cardiff case illustrates that it is not necessary to have an adolescent – never mind a young girl – at the centre of the activity. The participants were all mature adults. Secondly, if poltergeist activity represented the unbridled power of a mind in emotional turmoil, one would expect the results to exhibit chaos.

But in fact poltergeists seem to demonstrate an orderly intelligence, tuning in to the minds of those around them and responding accordingly, whether it is to frighten, amuse, or attempt to communicate.

Experts now believe that a poltergeist is either an intelligence that may once have been human, or more likely a non-human intelligence that feeds off the emotional energy of those around it, allowing it to manifest in our world.

How does the Cardiff case compare with other poltergeist manifestations? Professor David Fontana offered his thoughts: 'It's certainly one of the best cases the Society for Psychical Research has investigated, because of the number of reliable witnesses, the length of time, and because I saw many things myself. It would be very difficult to explain this case away. It does seem paranormal.'

8

THE HAUNTING OF BORLEY

T HE haunted house is perhaps the commonest and most popular theme in horror films and books. We are both fascinated and repelled by the prospect of a large rambling building with a brooding atmosphere and dark, bloody secrets.

The title 'most haunted house in England' is claimed by a number of places, including Abbey House in Cambridgeshire and Chingle Hall in Lancashire. But in the 1930s no one doubted that Borley Rectory in Essex should receive this dubious accolade. Was it haunted, or was it hype? And could it be that the village itself is still possessed by a supernatural agency, a force that moved to Borley church when the rectory was burnt down?

History and legend

The damp, draughty, redbrick rectory was built by the Revd Henry Bull in 1863. Its high gabled roofs, tall chimneys and tower crowded in with tall, gloomy trees made it look exactly how a haunted house should look. The village of Borley is so small that it lacks shop, post office and pub. Legend suggests that a monastery once existed where the rectory stood, but no evidence has been produced to support the idea. Stories that a secret tunnel connected Borley to a convent in the nearby village of Bures were given some credence when the council decided to put a water main in the village. During excavations a tunnel of sorts *was* discovered leading from the grounds of Borley Rectory and past the church before it petered out.

The original Borley church was constructed just after the Norman Conquest: twelfth-century flint and rubble have been discovered in the south wall of the nave. In the fifteenth and sixteenth centuries some rebuilding took place and the main structure was enlarged. The interior is dominated by a tomb belonging to the Waldegraves – who played their part in the story.

The strange sightings begin

The first recorded incidents were in 1885, at which time there were many accounts of an invisible coach and horses being heard on the road through Borley. A nurse called Mrs Byford was driven from the rectory on account of ghostly footsteps. During these early years the building was plagued by myriad claims of phenomena, including the padding of a dog, apparitions, amorphous shapes, the appearance of messages, apports, teleportation of objects, destruction of objects, and several sightings of a nun.

A SHOCK FOR THE SISTERS

The first real sighting was in broad daylight by the four sisters of the Revd Harry Bull, who succeeded his father in 1892. On the afternoon of 28 July 1900 Ethel, Freda and Mabel were returning from a garden party and chatting amicably as they entered the grounds of the rectory. Suddenly they noticed the figure of a young woman dressed as a nun. With bowed head, she was counting her Rosary beads as she walked – half glided – along the path between the trees and bushes.

Borley Rectory in Essex

The women, fear-struck, stood by the summer house watching the strangely garbed figure. They fetched another sister, Elsie. Now there were four witnesses to this amazing sight. Was it just someone dressed up as a prank? Elsie, determined to find out, moved towards the figure. The 'nun' turned her face towards Elsie. There was such an expression of intense grief written across it that Elsie almost stopped dead. At that moment the nun vanished.

Peter Underwood, investigator, author and President of the Ghost Club Society had the opportunity to interview the sisters about the sighting, and laid to rest the idea that ghosts are necessarily transparent amorphous phenomena: 'There are several things in this sighting that impress a modern parapsychologist. One is that the figure appeared to be absolutely normal. It looked solid, acted naturally and appeared to be real. Secondly, when approached it disappeared. These are the two main criteria that a parapsychologist requires to accept a sighting as genuine.'

The sisters had several other experiences at the rectory. In one of the passageways Ethel was confronted by a tall dark man who vanished in front of her. And several of the sisters watched a girl dressed in white walking towards the nearby River Stour, where she disappeared. This same apparition was apparently sighted nearly half a century later, in 1951, by a paranormal investigator.

'POACHERS'

The Revd Harry Bull also experienced his share of inexplicable happenings. One evening he was in the garden with his dog, Juvenal, when the retriever began howling and 'pointing' at some fruit trees. The rector moved closer and saw a pair of legs behind the foliage. Thinking he had disturbed a poacher, Bull skirted round to surprise the man. But it was just a pair of legs, and legs which could pass through a closed gate. The vicar also saw a wizened old man standing on the lawn, whom he recognised from old portraits as a family retainer who had died some two centuries before.

SERVANTS' TALES

Edward Cooper and his wife had many strange tales to tell during their long employ with the Bull family. Beginning in April 1916, almost every night they heard a sound like a large dog padding about coming from the kitchen. Finally, three years after the arrival of the phenomenon, the padding ended with a terrific crash like the breaking of china. The couple raced down to the kitchen – only to discover nothing out of place. The 'dog' never returned.

In the 1920s a Mrs Newman was employed as a cook. She always locked her bedroom door at night before retiring. Because her room was so large, a fine dividing curtain was hung down the middle. She slept in the half without a window; the other half had some pegs on the wall from which she hung her clothes. Several times, just as it was getting light, she was awakened by something. She could see her clothing being disturbed, silhouetted against the thin material of the curtain. As the light from the window increased, it was plain that something was moving between the curtain and the closed window. The young woman was too terrified to do anything.

'SISTERS OF MERCY'

After Harry Bull's death in 1927 the rectory lay empty for over a year. But people still claimed to experience things there. In the autumn of that year Fred Cartwright, a carpenter from nearby Sudbury, passed the house on his way to work one day just as it was getting light. He saw what he took to be a 'Sister of Mercy' standing by the rectory gate. She looked quite normal, but did not speak. The same thing happened on several subsequent occasions. Often the figure appeared to vanish inexplicably.

NEW RESIDENTS, NEW INVESTIGATIONS

In autumn 1928 the Revd Eric Smith and his wife moved in; their stay lasted just nine months. The doorbell would ring furiously when there was no one there. One night all the door keys fell out of their locks, then later vanished. Footsteps were heard about the house, small pebbles were thrown, lamps were lit, voices were heard, and Mrs Smith saw a phantom horse-drawn carriage standing in the drive. One day, she even found a skull, wrapped in brown paper in a cupboard.

In June 1929 the Revd Smith wrote to the Editor of the *Daily Mirror*, which had already run some stories on the rectory, asking him to recommend someone to look into the hauntings. The *Mirror* sent along a publicity-hungry psychic investigator, Harry Price. In the course of his lifetime Price carried out some important work exposing fake mediums and contributed greatly to psychical research; his extensive library is now housed at the University of London. It is ironic, then, that after his death, Price should have been accused of trickery and of hyping up the Borley saga.

During one visit to the rectory, Price had just descended the main staircase with a reporter when a candlestick hurtled down and shattered on the floor beside them. It was one of a pair they had just seen on the mantelpiece in one of the upstairs rooms. Next, a mothball hit the reporter on the hand.

GHOST VISITS TO A RECTORY

Tales of Headless Coachmen and a Lonely Nun

THE ELOPERS

Mysterious Happenings on Site of Old Monastery

FROM OUR SPECIAL CORRESPONDENT

LONG MELFORD, Sunday.

Ghostly figures of headless coachmen and a nun, an old-time coach, drawn by two bay horses, which appears and vanishes mysteriously, and dragging footsteps in empty rooms.

All these ingredients of a first class ghost story are awaiting investigation by psychic experts near Long Melford, Suffolk.

The scene of the ghostly visitations is the rectory at Borley, a few miles from Long Melford.

It is a building erected on the part of the site of a great monastery which, in the Middle Ages, was the scene of a gruesome tragedy.

The present rector, the Rev. G. E. Smith, and his wife, made the rectory their residence in the face of warnings by previous occupiers.

Since their arrival they have been puzzled and startled by a series of peculiar happenings which cannot be explained and which confirm the rumours they heard before moving in.

The first untoward happening was the sound of slow, dragging footsteps across the floor of an unoccupied room.

Then one night Mr. Smith, armed with a hockey stick, sat in the room and waited for the noise.

Once again it came—the sound of feet in some kind of slippers treading on the bare boards.

Mr. Smith lashed out with his stick at the spot where the footsteps seemed to be, but the stick whistled through the empty air, and the steps continued across the room.

Then a servant girl, brought from London, suddenly gave notice after two days' work, declaring emphatically that she had seen a nun walking in the wood at the back of the house.

Finally comes the remarkable story of an old-fashioned coach, seen twice on the lawn by a servant, which remained in sight long enough for the girl to distinguish the brown of the horses.

An extract from the Daily Mirror

(Harry Bull once declared that he would haunt the rectory by throwing mothballs.) This was followed by two showers of pebbles and a piece of slate.

Later that night Price organised a seance with the elderly Bull sisters and the Revd and Mrs Smith. An entity allegedly communicated with them by tapping on the back of a mirror. Using a code, it identified itself as Harry Bull, claiming he had been murdered!

After they left Borley, the publicity became too much and the Smiths tried to deny much of what they had claimed. Critics seized on this as proof that nothing much had happened.

The Foysters

Until 1929 the haunting had been benign, if at times scary. But with the arrival of the next incumbent, the Revd Lionel Algernon Foyster, together with his much younger wife Marianne and their adopted daughter Adelaide, a new wickedness crept into events.

Harry Price was at the house on one occasion when suddenly an empty claret bottle came rattling down the stairwell and smashed at his feet. Servant bells in the kitchen went berserk, and the bottle was followed by a shower of small pebbles. No one was upstairs at the time. A little later, Mrs Foyster cried out in alarm. She had been taking a nap in the bedroom and, although the door key had previously 'disappeared', discovered she was locked in. Price and the rector rushed upstairs. Apparently the Revd Foyster was used to this little problem. With the aid of a religious relic and much prayer, the lock mechanism snapped back and the door opened!

Harry Price, the Foysters and Mrs Goldney at the Rectory

A JP'S EXPERIENCES

Guy L'Estrange, a local headmaster and Justice of the Peace, visited the Foysters early in 1932 and afterwards reported what he saw and heard. The house revealed its nature to him immediately on arrival. As he was getting out of his car he noticed 'a tall figure standing quite still in the angle between the wall and the porch. It did not seem to be a shadow, though it [the light] was rather dim, and I called the driver's attention to the form.' As L'Estrange walked towards the figure, it vanished.

Shortly afterwards, taking tea with the rector and Mrs Foyster, he listened to the experiences of the vicar which he later wrote about in a local newspaper. '"I never believed in ghosts until I came here," said my host, "and used to laugh at the stories people told about this house. Since then I have discovered it is anything but a subject for laughter. One day while I was in my study," he declared, "I saw a pencil rise from my desk, and scrawl words on the wall. No hand was visible."' As the rector regaled his guest with further tales – of rooms being set on fire and of a jug being unaccountably thrown at him while he slept – they were all startled by a series of loud crashes and got up to investigate. L'Estrange again described the scene:

> Bottles were being hurled about in all directions in the hall, though nobody could be seen throwing them. Appearing suddenly in mid-air, they would hurtle through space and smash to pieces on the floor or against the wall...

The Haunted Rectory

Amazing Experiences of an Investigator

By GUY P. J. L'ESTRANGE

A GOOD many years have passed since my adventure in the "most haunted house in England," an account of which I broadcast several Christmases ago, but I have so often been asked to repeat the story that I need offer no apology for relating it here.

As much has been written in books and newspapers about that weird house since it was destroyed by fire, I am revealing no secret when I disclose that it was Borley Rectory, which stood near the border of Suffolk and Essex. It was in the early days of 1932 that the rector, hearing of my interest in haunted houses, invited me to visit him and give my opinion of the phenomena. I accepted gladly, for intriguing news of the uncanny happenings at the rectory had already been featured in the London Press, though care was taken to keep the whereabouts of the house a secret.

First Impressions

I arrived at the rectory in the early darkness of a January afternoon, and was immediately struck by its gloomy appearance. It was exactly the sort of place one associates with ghosts. A large old mansion (it was once the residence, I believe, of a well-known titled family), it had barred windows set in its grey walls, and a pinnacled tower stood on either side of the main doorway. The house was approached by a gravel drive, bordered with trees and shrubs, and I remembered that

so on. It was not very successful. True, a name was spelt out—a name which was known to the householders—but after that the bells fell silent, and we returned to the drawing-room. "I am certain there are devils at the back of these disturbances," insisted the rector.

A little later I sat alone before the fire, while the rector attended to some work in his study and his wife helped her maid to prepare supper. With a small oil-lamp by my side I was making notes of the evening's happenings, when I heard cautious footsteps enter the room. A chill ran down my spine, but I did not look round until the footsteps paused behind the settee on which I was seated. Then I turned quickly. There was nobody to be seen, but the footsteps passed on and seemed to go through the wall at the far end of the room. I learned later that there had formerly been a door in that part of the wall.

The Noise on the Stairs

Space forbids me to give details of everything I saw and heard during that eventful night, but I must mention a curious incident which happened after supper. I was talking to my hostess in the dark hall, when she interrupted me with a soft "Hush," and I heard the sound of laboured breathing on the stairs. We stood listening for about half-a-minute, and then I suddenly flashed my electric torch. No other night but the noise

An extract from Guy L'Estrange's article

The Rector explained that they had been stored in a shed outside, but could not tell me how they got into the house. 'You see,' he said, 'the doors are locked, and every window is bolted.'

Afterwards they toured the house to point out to the visitor where other strange phenomena had occurred. 'As we went onto the landing there was a loud ringing of bells downstairs ... I could see all the bells in the kitchen passage below were clanging wildly at the same time, while my hostess and the one maid who had not refused to remain in the house looked on helplessly.' There were some thirty bells ringing, yet the rector explained to L'Estrange that the wires of all but three had previously been cut. L'Estrange's account continued:

At my hostess' suggestion, I tried to communicate with the unseen entity responsible. 'If,' I cried, looking up at the bells, 'some invisible person is present and can hear my words, please stop those bells ringing for a moment.' Instantly, every bell became still. I do not mean that they gradually slowed down, as one would expect. It was as though each had been seized and held by a hidden hand.

Previously, an attempt at exorcism had only intensified the phenomena. One night the rector's wife was thrown out of bed three times by an unseen force.

MORE WRITING ON THE WALL

During this period, Marianne Foyster became more and more the focus for the strange, unbelievable power that seemed to have Borley Rectory in its grip. Messages appeared on the walls addressed to 'Marianne', asking for 'light', 'mass' and 'prayers'. Was this an earth-bound soul asking for deliverance, or a further example of a massive fraud? The words were written in a scrawling hand, unintelligible at times. Underneath, Mrs Foyster would reply in block letters: 'I CANNOT UNDERSTAND, TELL ME MORE.' Later, more writing would appear below this. On one occasion, Mrs Foyster and a visiting priest, Dom Edwin Whitehouse, knelt down and asked where the mass should be offered. The word 'here' appeared on the wall.

As the investigation proceeded, many of those involved began to formulate the idea that the messenger was the same entity who had been sighted around the grounds dressed as a nun. But how could that apparition be linked with the more violent goings-on in the rectory itself? Apart from the smashing of crockery and bottles, there were the physical attacks.

Messages addressed to 'Marianne' appeared on the walls

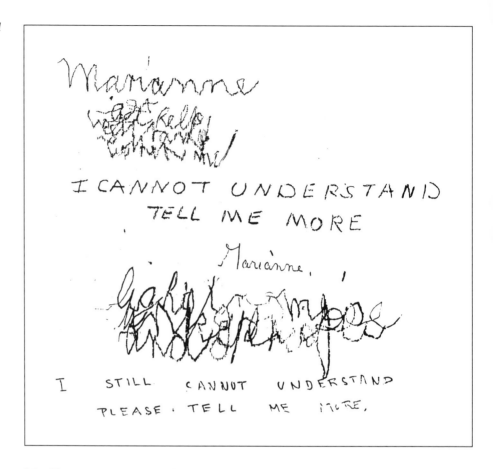

Mrs Foyster was once walking along a passage when something struck her a terrific blow under the eye, causing heavy bleeding. The damaged eye was black for several days. On another occasion she was struck on the back by a piece of pottery which again drew blood.

The conclusion was drawn that there were two types of entities operating in the rectory, benevolent ones and cruel ones. The Foysters left Borley in October 1935, and later an incredible story was to emerge about their private lives.

Romance and murder

Helen Glanville and her brother, Squadron-Leader Roger Glanville, were among many investigators attempting to shed light on the strange phenomena. Through their seances a story began to emerge, albeit accompanied by much contradictory and nonsensical information.

The 'nun' stated that she was unhappy but would be content if she had a Christian burial. But where were the remains? The sitters were offered a variety of locations. She was buried in the garden, near the house, near a path, under some trees, but not under a stone. They were finally informed that she was buried under a stone in the garden path. All of this was gleaned during two seances held on 23 and 25 October 1937.

It was several days later that Helen Glanville decided to try the planchette (see box below) – a device she had never used before. The results were so extensive that they were recorded on rolls of wallpaper! An examination of the writing indicated that the nun's name was 'Mary Lairre' and she had come over from a nunnery somewhere near 'Havre' in France. The entity also made mention of 'Marianne'. She asked for a mass to be held, and communicated the date of her death – 17 May 1667, when she was just nineteen. The reason for her unhappiness was that someone called 'Walde-grave' had strangled her after enticing her away from her native France. The

CONTACTING DISCARNATE ENTITIES

There are several methods by which people think they may be able to contact so-called discarnate entities.

The planchette is an automatic writing device and consists of a large board with a sheet of paper over it. A heart-shaped piece of wood mounted on castors sits on this, through which a pencil makes contact with the paper. The operators each rest a finger on the contraption. An entity can then supposedly communicate with the sitters by operating through them, forcing the pencil to move on the paper.

A variation on the planchette is the ouija board. This consists of the letters of the alphabet arranged in a circle on a polished board. In the centre rests an upturned glass. The sitters each place a finger on the glass, and in response to questions, it moves around the board spelling out replies.

In some cases the investigators can persuade the entity to tap out responses to questions. One tap means 'no', two indicates 'don't know', and three 'yes'.

Spiritualist mediums call up entities during seances. Often they are aided in this by guides in the spirit world. The medium relates mess-ages which are communicated to her. Sometimes the entity allegedly takes over the body of the medium, and speaks directly to the sitters.

In the early days of spiritualism physical mediums were able to materialise entities using a substance called ectoplasm. There are lots of photographs of ectoplasm, said to be alive and sensitive to light and touch. Mediums claimed to produce it from their mouths, ears and noses. Most of those who were investigated turned out to be frauds.

Waldegraves were an old family who had once owned Borley and the surrounding area. Had these events really taken place?

There was a lot of 'information' given by 'Mary Lairre' which turned out to be factually inaccurate and blatantly contradictory. Yet through the smoke screens and background 'chatter' emerged a story. A Waldegrave had taken the young novice away from her convent and installed her at Borley as his mistress. Something had gone drastically wrong with the relationship and Waldegrave had strangled the girl, burying her body somewhere in the grounds or beneath the house; there were several references to a blocked-up well in the cellar. But 'Mary Lairre' was not the only entity to communicate with the investigators.

In broken sentences, an 'entity' calling itself 'Sunex Amures' said that the rectory would be destroyed by fire that night, and beneath the ruins they would find some bones which were the source of the haunting. This seance took place in Streatham, London on 27 March 1938. But there was no fire that night. The burning was to come exactly eleven months later, on 27 February 1939, and the remains of a woman were indeed discovered under the ruins.

Burial of the 'Borley Nun' by Revd A C Henning

Many people gathered to watch the destruction of the rectory, and some of them, including a policeman, claimed to have seen strange figures moving amongst the flames.

On 29 May 1945, the remains which had been discovered after the fire were given a Christian burial in nearby Liston churchyard by the Revd A C Henning, with Price in attendance.

The price of success

After the death in 1948 of the most celebrated of the investigators, Harry Price, the knives came out. Charles Sutton of the *Daily Mail* claimed that during a visit in 1929 he had caught Price with pebbles in his pocket – after one had hit the reporter on the head. Price was an accomplished amateur conjuror, and his critics used this to support their belief that he was responsible for many of the 'phenomena'. While Borley Rectory lay in ruins, Price had visited it with a magazine photographer. One of the photographs showed what Price claimed was a brick suspended in mid-air. What he did not say was that at the time workmen were demolishing a wall nearby.

The academics of the Society of Psychical Research had never been comfortable with Harry Price's flirtations with the media and his opportunist attitude towards self-publicity. Two of them, Lord Charles Hope and Major Henry Douglas-Home, said they had grave doubts about the phenomena

The infamous 'suspended brick' photograph

they had witnessed at Borley in the company of Price. As a result, an investigation of the evidence was ordered, to be conducted by Mrs K M Goldney, Dr Eric Dingwall and Trevor Hall. In 1956 the results were published under the title *The Haunting of Borley Rectory*.

The book largely blamed Harry Price for creating a living legend that he exploited to the full and indeed contributed to with acts of trickery. This included his 'discovery' of the bones of a woman in the rectory cellar, which his critics claimed Price had planted there. On this edifice of deception he had written two best-selling books: *The Most Haunted House in England* and *The End of Borley Rectory*.

TRICKERY OR JUST EXAGGERATION?

Charles Wintour is a former Editor of the London *Evening Standard*. In 1938, as a Cambridge undergraduate, he answered an advertisement by Price, asking for volunteers to help him solve the mystery. Price had rented the empty rectory for a year after the Revd and Marianne Foyster left. Wintour did not trust Price, but thinks he was exaggerating things rather than inventing them.

'I went to Borley with an entirely open mind. As far as I could make out there were manifestations occurring. It wasn't at all frightening. We took

The advertisement placed by Price in **The Times**

precautions to make sure no one could enter rooms or passages by placing cotton strands across the entrances. But pencil marks started appearing on the walls. We would circle each mark and time and date them – but new ones kept appearing. On one occasion I saw a pencil mark apparently moving along a wall until it trailed off.'

Alan Wesencraft is the curator of the Harry Price Library at the University of London. He met Price and sums him up in these words: 'Harry Price struck me as a man who had tremendous enthusiasm. But I think this led him into making exaggerated claims. He had a fertile imagination and this would take charge. However, basically, I'm sure he was honest, and didn't wilfully lead people astray.'

The odd couple

In the Foysters' time at Borley, Price made just one visit, in October 1931. He told the Revd Foyster that in his opinion Marianne was responsible for much of the 'poltergeist' activity. It was subsequently discovered that the lives of Lionel Foyster and his young wife read like something from a sleazy soap opera. Trevor Hall had pursued the story of Marianne in the 1950s. Then Robert Wood who was brought up not far from Borley, took up where Hall had left off. With the help of her adopted son, John Fisher, he produced a remarkable book called *The Widow of Borley*.

In it, he rejects the idea that paranormal events might be involved. He refers to the Society for Psychical Research as 'a farcical organisation', and in moral outrage talks of Lionel Foyster as 'a country parson who was also a Cambridge graduate, a sexual deviant and a liar'. Marianne 'was not only a fraud but a pathological liar' who, according to Wood, probably murdered Foyster. Wood finds something derogatory to say about almost everyone. His attitude must be borne in mind, therefore, when evaluating some of his more speculative conclusions.

UNUSUAL RELATIONSHIPS

Lionel Algernon Foyster first met his future wife when he was a curate at Oughtrington near Lymm in Cheshire. He baptised her on 19 June 1906 when she was seven years old. The Revd Foyster was already on friendly terms with the family and, according to Wood, became 'obsessed' with the little girl. When she was eleven Foyster moved to Canada. In 1914, Marianne became pregnant and married a man called Greenwood. Just weeks after the birth, Greenwood absconded. According to the child, Ian, his mother then embarked on a series of affairs.

When the Revd Foyster wrote to Marianne in 1922 proposing marriage, she accepted. The forty-four-year-old clergyman did not know of her previous marriage nor of the existence of the child, who was introduced as Marianne's brother. She joined Foyster in Canada, and eight years later they returned to England.

According to Ian, who hated his mother, Marianne continued her affairs in Canada. At Borley she installed one of her lovers in the adjoining cottage, François d'Arles (real name Frank Pearless) and his son. He spent a lot of time at the rectory, even sleeping there. Wood reasons that Foyster not only knew about his wife's infidelities, but encouraged them. In 1933 she and Pearless opened a florist's shop in Wimbledon, South London, and posed as man and wife, visiting the rectory at weekends. When the business failed nearly two years later, the relationship broke up.

BIGAMY IN IPSWICH

The story becomes even more incredible when we hear that Marianne was then installed in rented rooms in Ipswich, posing as a single woman. Marianne knew they would soon have to leave Borley because of Lionel's deteriorating health, and would then have very little to live on. Wood conjectures that Marianne was in Ipswich to ensnare a breadwinner. The victim was a mentally unstable commercial traveller named Henry Fisher, to whom Foyster was introduced as Marianne's father! After Marianne and Fisher married in February 1935, Foyster left the rectory and went to live with them.

While still 'married' she allegedly had another affair, then started up relations with Robert O'Neil, a US serviceman. Fisher eventually left her and had a nervous breakdown. Foyster was now bedridden, and died on 18 April 1945. Trevor Hall and Robert Wood were both convinced that Marianne played an active role in his death. Next she married the much younger Robert O'Neil and emigrated to America.

A genuine poltergeist exploited?

What have the private lives of the Foysters to do with the alleged haunting of the rectory? According to critics, this information is crucial. Many cases of paranormal phenomena stand or fall by the reputation of the witnesses, and both the Foysters spent their lives in a series of lies.

The haunting was at its worst during the period when they were resident at Borley. Wood conjectures that Foyster, Marianne and Pearless were continually playing cruel and malicious 'poltergeist' tricks on one another. The black eyes which Marianne sported were caused not by genuine phenomena, but by her lover during their many rows. The writing on the walls, allegedly from the nun, compared well with Marianne's own handwriting. Lionel Foyster, like Eric Smith before him, hoped to write a best-selling book on the haunting – which gave the motivation for the pretence.

Many sceptics have written off Borley Rectory as a total sham, but in truth that does not wash. Phenomena were recorded well before the Smiths or the Foysters, and have continued since. From a parapsychologist's point of view, it is no surprise that the phenomena grew more violent and intense during the Foyster years. Poltergeists are usually reported in situations of extreme emotional energy. There was certainly plenty of that at Borley Rectory in what Wood called 'an atmosphere of mutual suspicion, sexual jealousy and obsessive love'.

Dom Edwin Whitehouse was questioned by paranormal investigator Peter Underwood about his visits to the rectory. 'He was quite convinced that Marianne had experienced things for which she was not responsible. There were a number of occasions where he claimed bottles materialised in front of his eyes.'

When she was seven, Pamela Bullock visited the rectory with her mother and grandmother. She remembers going into a large room with her grandmother when suddenly a face appeared at the window. It was in black, like a habit. They fled in terror.

If there *was* paranormal activity in and around the house it was built on and embellished by human players with a vested interest in bringing it to the attention of others. Pencil marks might have paranormally appeared on walls, but it is unlikely that any entity wrote in Marianne Foyster's handwriting. When the rectory burned down, it may have been nothing to do with 'Sunex Amures'; there were suspicions of arson by the last owner, although these were never proved and the insurance company did partially pay out.

But even if the hundreds of eye-witness reports are branded as imagination and lies, this does not explain the phenomena recorded across the road at Borley church.

Borley church

In 1929 Ethel Bull told Harry Price of an incident in the nineteenth century when coffins in the Waldegrave vault beneath the church were discovered to have been moved. Is the entire *place* of Borley haunted, and not just the rectory? The church has not suffered from the hype associated with its infamous former neighbour, so perhaps the claims about it can be better assessed.

During the 1960s a small group of researchers from Harlow in Essex conducted a series of late night vigils. They heard bangs, knocks and the sound of heavy furniture being moved around. During one attempt to record the noises the group found their tape recorder smashed, with the tape torn from its reel. In the early hours they heard 'laughter and merriment which seemed to be coming up the road towards Borley Church'. Yet there was no one on the road, and a search of the area by car drew a blank.

In the orchard opposite the church they were allegedly confronted by something huge and dark 'like an animal' which banged loudly on the fence. Investigators Geoffrey Croom-Hollingsworth and Roy Potter also claim to have seen the nun. According to Croom-Hollingsworth: 'Suddenly I saw her quite clearly, in a grey habit and cowl as she moved across the garden and through a hedge.' Then the figure disappeared into a garage, and he wondered if it was a hoax. He called out to Potter, and they both saw the 'nun' reappear through the far wall of the garage. 'She approached to about twelve feet from us, and we both saw her face, that of an elderly woman in her sixties, perhaps. We followed her as she seemed to glide over a dry ditch as if it wasn't there, before she disappeared into a pile of building bricks.'

GRUNTS, SIGHS AND PHANTOM ORGAN-PLAYING

In 1974 film director Denny Densham obtained permission to carry out a series of vigils in the church using sophisticated recording equipment. The machines picked up unidentified noises and the unmistakable sound of a heavy door being opened and slammed shut, with the squeaking of a rusty bolt.

On a further visit the equipment was set up and a search of the building made as normal. Half the team were locked inside and the rest remained in the churchyard. 'Suddenly,' Densham said, 'there was a curious change in the atmosphere. One of the team felt as if he was being watched, and we all felt very cold.'

On the tapes were the usual knockings and rappings, and the crash of the door again. A tape in one small cassette machine was discovered to have been unravelled, but on a second a human sigh was clearly recorded. On other occasions heavy footsteps were picked up, even though the stone floor is carpeted. Finally, the team saw a glow of light by the chancel door and heard a horrible grunt.

Members of a parapsychical group from Enfield in Middlesex also heard strange noises and a deep grunting voice, as founder member Ron Russell attests: 'One night in July 1980, myself and three colleagues locked six tape recorders inside the church. Amongst the unidentified sounds we recorded a very loud bang, as if something had been thrown down on the stone floor

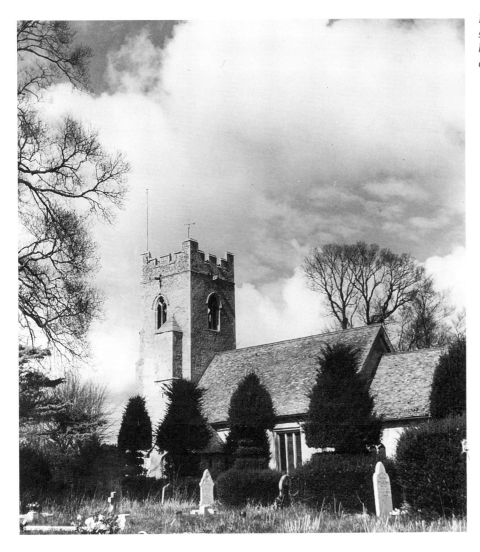

Borley Church where strange phenomena have been experienced

around the altar. There was also a strange guttural voice, or growling, which is very scary. I've no doubt in my mind that these sounds were paranormal.'

Although there has been no major investigation of Borley in recent years, people still have strange experiences. Pamela Bullock was visiting the church with her husband Frederick and daughter Lucille one lunchtime in the 1980s. 'Before we went into the church we heard what sounded like an organ playing – it was rather beautiful. As we entered, the music stopped. There was not a soul in the church and the organ console was padlocked. I stood in the central aisle facing the altar, to the right of the Waldegrave tomb. Suddenly we were aware of the sound of pebbles falling, or being thrown, on to the floor of the altar. It was very distinctive, but we couldn't find any evidence of pebbles.'

This is only one of many incidents. Geoff Brown followed them over the years as editor of the *Suffolk Free Press*. Does he think there is a rational explanation?

'So many things happened at Borley over such a long period of time that there's never been a satisfactory explanation. I've been involved with Borley as a journalist and editor for forty years, and in every one of those years things have been reported. I think something was there. Borley will always remain the most haunted place in England.'

UFOs AND
CLOSE ENCOUNTERS

As the space age has taken off, so too have reports of UFOs and alien encounters. They've become perhaps the greatest mystery of today. Is the earth a lonely planet in an intergalactic void, or is the universe teeming with life – some of which may travel to our world? And why do UFO sightings focus in certain places? So-called 'window' areas may reveal secrets far removed from little green men in flying saucers. But there are few cases like the amazing close encounter in an English pine forest; quite simply regarded as the most important ever to occur in the British Isles, and one of the most dramatic anywhere in the world. This story has everything, from official recognition to physical evidence, and will challenge even the most sceptical. Do we finally have that elusive proof that *they* are here; that we *do* share our earth with visitors from somewhere else?

9
THE BONNYBRIDGE UFO WINDOW

SOMEWHERE on this planet an unidentified flying object is sighted once every two or three minutes. Witnesses on every continent, in every country are spotting odd things in the sky which they are quite unable to explain. But nowhere, it seems, more than the small Scottish town of Bonnybridge.

Strange sightings – reluctant witnesses

UFO researchers – or UFOlogists as they are known – believe that only one in ten, perhaps as few as one in a hundred sightings are ever made public. Reasons cited by reluctant observers emphasise the fear of ridicule; for, despite rising levels of interest in the subject, it is still considered rather a social stigma to have witnessed a phenomenon that, according to logic, ought not to be there. So most people choose to remain silent.

However, it is much easier to be brave when you are in the company of others. So if an area achieves local notoriety as a hotspot for UFO activity, formerly reticent witnesses may well come into the open and admit that they saw something extraordinary. This process quickly becomes self-perpetuating, fuelling new publicity and further sighting reports.

WINDOWS ON TO THE UNKNOWN

The situation is also complicated by the fact that in some parts of the world, claims of UFO sightings are far more frequent than chance dictates. These places have been conferred with the name UFO 'windows': in them, given the number of reports, there is a much greater than usual chance of seeing something truly astonishing.

Most such windows were established by a track record of sightings throughout the ages – indeed back into the distant past long before words like 'UFO' or 'alien' were invented. It is rare for a new window to appear, or to be discovered, seemingly out of nowhere, but in late 1992 that is just what happened in and around Bonnybridge. Indeed, this once quiet spot is now widely regarded as a UFO hotspot – a true haven for skygazers the world over.

UFO WINDOWS AROUND THE WORLD

More than a hundred window areas have been identified around the world, from the Brazilian rainforest to the Australian outback. Some notable examples are:

- The hills of south-west Texas. An orange-coloured ball of light known as the Marfa Light has been reported here for centuries, first by native American tribes and pioneer settlers, nowadays by locals and tourists.

- Hessdalen, a narrow valley near Trondheim in northern Norway. Radar, laser tracking systems and sophisticated film techniques have been used to research the multi-coloured light phenomena. Evidence suggests they are a kind of plasma, but they are also said to respond to human thoughts and actions. (See photograph facing page 128).

- Britain's most intense window is in the Pennine hills, around Leeds, Manchester and Sheffield. Police have confirmed chasing low-level UFOs over the moors and there are local stories of a 'mystery helicopter'. The strange objects often land in and take off from quarries, giving rise to rumours of underground bases deep within the rock.

The Bonnybridge window opens

Bonnybridge is sited on the Firth of Forth, an estuary north-west of Edinburgh. Aside from nearby moderate-sized towns such as Larbert, Cumbernauld, Livingston and Falkirk, it comprises mostly hilly countryside with widely scattered villages.

The area first came to prominence in November 1992 when Billy Buchanan, a local councillor, received a visitor whilst he was watching TV. It was a local businessman, whom Buchanan knew very well. Dishevelled and upset, the visitor told him about a strange object which had hovered above the road for about ten minutes before suddenly shooting off.

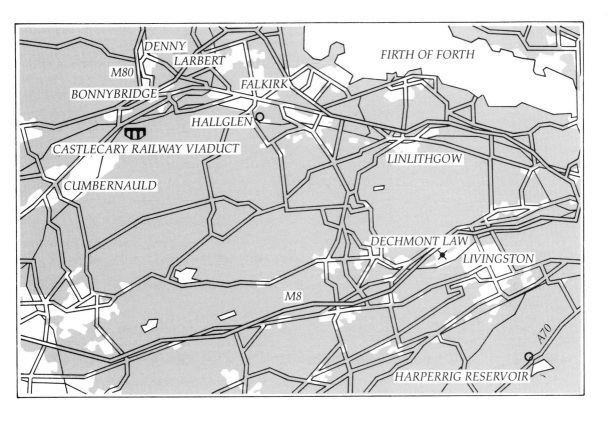

A map of the Bonnybridge area

Buchanan suggested calling the police, but the man did not want the likely publicity – he had just needed to tell someone about what he had witnessed. So the councillor decided to take the pressure off the troubled man and report the sighting to the local media on his behalf, appealing for other witnesses to come forward. He was amazed at the response. Within three days he received over 150 phone and personal calls from people stating that they had seen something strange in the sky.

Of course, a number of these cases were quite old and most were just accounts of lights in the sky which could well have been mundane objects such as aircraft lights or meteors. However, a family did describe a huge blue light that landed on the road dead ahead of them near Hallglen in March 1992. Local UFOlogists were particularly excited when they heard about Councillor Buchanan's one-man UFO crusade.

Still the sightings poured in – around eight hundred of them by mid-1994. They told of 'a silver cylinder hovering in the sky', 'a circle of revolving lights', 'a glowing ball with fuzzy edges' and 'a giant Toblerone bar hanging in mid-air,' plus many other wondrous things.

Before long most of the townsfolk had either seen a UFO or knew someone who had. The attention of the UFO world was now fixed on Scotland.

'I saw what I saw ...'

A typical report from the Bonnybridge area is that of Ray and Kathy Procek, who were driving west on the M80 motorway south of Denny at 8.25pm on 16 January 1993. They were approaching the spot where they had to drive underneath the Castlecary railway viaduct.

Mrs Procek, who was driving, was the first to spot a series of lights in the sky, which she pointed out to her husband. They were not flashing but seemed to be studded on the outside of a large oval craft.

Mr Procek, not having to concentrate on the road, was able to take a long look at the object. As they got closer he could make out the shape: the back end, he says, was elliptical, and as their car passed beneath they saw that it was triangular. When they emerged on the far side of the viaduct a second, identical object was sitting in the sky – seemingly pointed straight at the first one.

The couple quickly ruled out aircraft or helicopters, due to the lack of motion or sound. As they drove away, with the craft still there, they were completely mystified but decided not to report what they had seen. The story only emerged later because their son was loosely connected with a Scottish UFO group and passed the information to them.

Kathy Procek says: 'I don't know what it was that I saw – like nothing that I have seen before. I am quite willing to believe that there is something out there.'

Her husband, mindful that their son's involvement with a UFO group might spoil their credibility as dispassionate witnesses, noted: 'I have no reason to make up this story. I saw what I saw and it's as simple as that.'

A very close encounter

It is not only strange lights and fantastic objects that are being sighted in the Bonnybridge area – there are also what UFO investigators call close encounters. An incident reported by two young men, Colin Wright and Garry Wood, was clearly very frightening indeed.

At 11.35pm one night in August 1992 they were driving along an isolated section of the A70 near Harperrig Reservoir up in the Pentland Hills. As they rounded a blind corner they were astonished to find an object blocking their path.

Colin says: 'There was a craft approximately 20 feet above us.' Garry, who was driving, adds: 'It was about 30 feet wide and black in colour ... When I saw the object I got such a fright that I pushed down hard on the accelerator.' The car lurched forward, rushing into the acute bend at more than 40 mph.

THE OZ FACTOR

At this point several things happened at once. The car had a CD player which was on at the time, but as they passed beneath the hovering object the volume of the music faded noticeably.

The two men also experienced a strange sensation nicknamed by UFOlogists the 'Oz factor' after the fairytale reality of *The Wizard of Oz*. In this condition a witness will describe how the sounds of the environment disappear, how their mind becomes disorientated and they seemingly enter an altered state of consciousness. Their sense of the passage of time is also commonly affected.

However, the most terrifying aspect of the two men's close encounter concerned the incredible black mass directly overhead. Garry recalls: 'As I accelerated underneath it this shimmering curtain appeared from nowhere beneath the craft.' They were already too close to avoid driving straight into it, but within moments of doing so they found themselves enveloped in total darkness, seemingly due to the UFO's shroud.

Everything in the car went black, say the two, and the road and surrounding area completely disappeared. Colin adds: 'I kept thinking that we were going to crash into a field, because there was another tight bend after this first one. But for some reason we did not do so. The next thing I remember is a big jolt from the back of the car.' They did not look back, and fled from the scene in fright.

An extract from the questionnaire filled in by Colin Wright for the British UFO Research Association, including a sketch of the 'object'

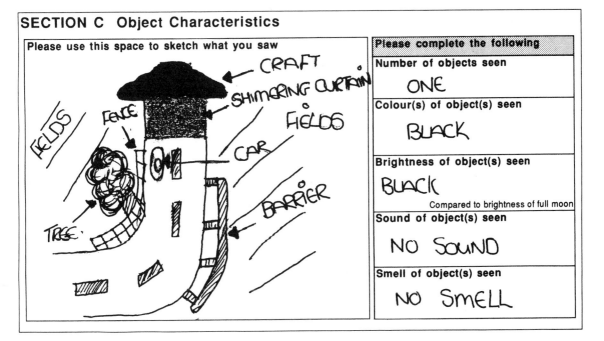

SECTION C Object Characteristics

Please use this space to sketch what you saw

CRAFT
SHIMMERING CURTAIN
FIELDS
CAR
BARRIER
FENCE
FIELDS
TREE

Please complete the following

Number of objects seen
ONE

Colour(s) of object(s) seen
BLACK

Brightness of object(s) seen
BLACK
Compared to brightness of full moon

Sound of object(s) seen
NO SOUND

Smell of object(s) seen
NO SMELL

4) Where were you at the time of the incident?
including nearest street, town or village

ON THE A70 JUST PAST HARPERIGS RESERVOIR

5) What first brought your attention to the object(s)?

OBJECT WAS FLOATING IN FRONT OF CAR,

6) How did the object(s) disappear from view?

DROVE UNDERNEATH THE OBJECT CANT REMEMBER
ANYTHING ELSE.

Further details from Colin Wright's questionnaire

Logically they should have mounted the steep embankment of the bend and had a serious accident. However, they emerged from this bizarre confrontation perfectly all right. Indeed, the car was aligned correctly on the road but they were now an unknown distance further along their route, with no memory of how they had escaped the UFO's clutches or its shimmering curtain spread all around them. They also had no idea just how they had avoided catastrophe, driving blind in the pitch-dark surroundings.

For the rest of the night the two men felt very peculiar, as if drugged. They had been on their way to visit friends, and when they arrived each man independently made a nearly identical sketch of the black mass. The terror etched on their faces was all that was required to convince their hosts that this was no joke.

The two men have since driven up on to the moors with a video camera, shooting the fields, hills and reservoir – just waiting and hoping. As yet they have encountered nothing else, but their lives have been irrevocably altered by those few moments of terror on that dangerous bend. Indeed, even now they are undergoing hypnotherapy in the hope of discovering what else might have happened during those few moments of time.

Caught on camera

With so many sightings in the area it was inevitable that someone would capture something on camera. That moment arrived at about 7pm on 19 January 1994, when twenty-seven-year-old Neil Malcolm was driving home from his aunt's house in Larbert.

Neil spotted a bright white light moving towards him, and then became concerned when a beam of light illuminated the interior of his Vauxhall Nova. He put his foot down and reached home within a few minutes, rushing inside to tell his wife, brother, sister-in-law and parents who were all together in the house.

At first they thought Neil was joking, but they quickly realised how shocked he was and hurried outside. Here they all saw the object for themselves. The light was closer now and at one point resolved itself into a cylindrical shape, but for most of the time it remained just an intense white light. It continued on its silent downward path above a bus garage.

Lorraine Malcolm, Neil's wife, ran back inside to collect her video camera. She had to insert a battery and set it up, but she arrived outside again in time to see the light dropping behind the building. It was moving in fits and starts, slowing down and then speeding up again. She managed to catch about 18 seconds of its flight.

UFOlogists were alerted by Billy Buchanan and checked out local airports. There was an inbound plane from Aberdeen that might have been in the area, but this seems difficult to equate with what appeared on Lorraine's videotape. There is no sign of any flashing navigation lights, for example.

An alien assault

Undoubtedly the most well-known case in the Bonnybridge area dates back to well before the current mystery began. It occurred in November 1979 on a damp morning near Dechmont Law, a forested area close to the M8 motorway at Livingston.

Forestry worker Bob Taylor was on patrol with his dog, checking for stray sheep, when he says he came upon a strange object sitting on the ground or hovering just above it. A line of rotating arms were set into a rim surrounding the circular object and it was fading in and out of view, allowing background trees to be visible – almost as if it were attempting to camouflage itself.

Bob Taylor describes how he stared in amazement as two metal spheres with spikes on, not unlike sea mines, emerged from the rear of the object and bounced towards him. They made horrible, sucking noises as they impacted into the wet soil. As they reached his side he became aware of a curious acrid smell, then felt a tugging on his legs and collapsed unconscious on to the ground.

The forester recovered an unknown time later – estimates suggest it was fifteen or twenty minutes. Nothing was now visible in the clearing, but his

A artist's impression of the craft Taylor described, based on sketches he drew after the assault

dog was running about barking and yapping, prompting speculation that it had frightened off the intruders. Taylor was weak and dizzy and could not stand, but he dragged himself to his vehicle at the edge of the clearing. However, his co-ordination was seriously awry and he drove into a ditch.

Taylor eventually reached his home at the edge of the woods having partly dragged himself and then stumbled through the undergrowth. His wife saw at once that he had been attacked, which he confirmed. But – he added sombrely – his assailants were not exactly human.

Mrs Taylor rang Malcolm Drummond, Taylor's boss, who arrived at the house to hear his story, even though the man was dazed, had a headache and kept saying that he had been 'gassed'. A doctor was called and Taylor was sent to hospital, although he checked himself out later without being examined.

Meanwhile, Taylor's employers at the Livingston New Town Development Corporation had been called in to investigate, as had the police. They were not laughing but were treating the matter as a physical assault by person or persons unknown – a prospect then unprecedented in UFO history.

Bob Taylor at the site of the encounter

Drummond arranged to meet the police at the clearing. Here they found Taylor's vehicle and also, as Drummond notes, 'marks on the ground which seemed to indicate that something had come vertically down and made impressions in the turf'. These resembled a bulldozer or heavy machinery, but surrounding them were forty shallow holes that matched the witness's story about the bouncing spiky balls.

The police fenced off the area and were utterly baffled, since the tracks covered only this one area of grass. There was no indication of how the vehicle that caused them had arrived.

SECRET WEAPONRY?

Malcolm Drummond is adamant about the physical evidence that he saw: 'There is no doubt in my mind that these marks were made by a perfectly solid, heavier-than-air object. They had been made by some machine which had come vertically downward ... I don't believe in anything from outer space. The only conclusion that I can come to is that it must have been a man-made object ... some sort of secret machine belonging to one of the government departments.'

Detective Sergeant Ian Wark was a member of the police team assigned to the case. He admits that he was highly sceptical when first sent to the scene, but on examining the forty holes and the weird caterpillar tracks he was puzzled. He checked all the forestry equipment used in the area; none of it had tracks that matched. After the investigation Wark was in no doubt. 'In my opinion,' he said, 'Mr Taylor genuinely reported what he saw, or believed that he had seen.'

The police sent Bob Taylor's trousers to Edinburgh for forensic analysis. Lester Knibb, a forensic scientist in the laboratory, found clear tear marks on either side, consistent with the witness's story about being grabbed at waist height by the two spiky sea mines. The police lab could not prove anything, but Knibb says: 'The damage could have been caused in the way the witness says. But it would require something mechanical. It was not something caused by an electric shock or bolt of lightning.' These were theories that sceptics were proposing at the time.

Detective Sergeant Wark confirms: 'We are still baffled ... the case is still open.'

A SPI on the sky

SPI – Strange Phenomena Investigations – is one of Scotland's best-known UFO investigation groups. It is co-ordinated by Malcolm Robinson, an experienced researcher, editor of *Enigmas* magazine and regional coordinator of investigations for BUFORA, the British UFO Research Association.

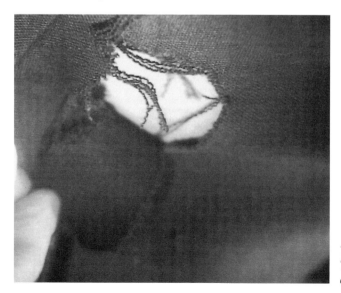

The tear marks on Bob Taylor's trousers were carefully examined

He first heard about the Bonnybridge sightings during a radio broadcast and contacted Billy Buchanan to offer advice. A close rapport developed between the two men, and they were frequently cited by the local press as the campaign grew to uncover further sightings.

In January 1993 Buchanan organised a public meeting for residents of Bonnybridge to try to alleviate their escalating concern. Some three hundred people attended and quizzed SPI members or told their stories to one another.

Throughout 1993 the media surge continued. Americans arrived to send back film reports to TV stations at home. A team of Japanese researchers collated film about the town for transmission to an audience of 23 million. All this led to a decision to organise a UFO conference in nearby Falkirk, hosted jointly by Buchanan and Robinson. Held in June 1994, it attracted over six hundred local people and was the most successful UFO event ever held in Scotland. Clearly the fascination with the Bonnybridge window shows no sign of abating and, if anything, is actually on the increase.

Malcolm Robinson's team check with police, airports and other establishments and find that nine times out of ten there is a perfectly rational explanation to account for UFO reports. These resolved cases include some from Bonnybridge, but he adds: 'There is a residue of unexplainable reports coming from this area which, as yet, we just cannot identify ... These cases are very, very unusual. They are low-level, close-proximity UFO observations which do not conform to any conventional type of aircraft or helicopter ... At the end of the day such UFO reports demand serious investigation.' This work, he says, will go on and they look at all serious theories – even those from sceptics.

The sceptic's viewpoint

Some authorities, however, question the existence of the Bonnybridge 'window' and the strange nature of the Bob Taylor landing. The most outspoken of these is Steuart Campbell, a former BUFORA investigator who actually compiled the Association's case history on the Livingston incident in 1979. At that time he proposed the idea that Bob Taylor might have encountered ball lightning, a rare atmospheric effect which rendered him unconscious; but he has changed his opinions on that possibility.

In 1994 – now a freelance sceptic and fresh from demystifying the Loch Ness Monster – Campbell published his controversial book *The UFO Mystery – Solved!*, in which he proposed a dramatic new theory to explain both the Livingston case in particular and UFOs in general. He believes they are caused by astronomical mirages.

He notes that, although the police did not find whatever machinery caused the tracks in Dechmont Woods, he is certain that it was something quite ordinary. He claims that, having trained as an architect and therefore familiar with the effects of heavy plant machinery on the ground of building sites, he could see how the grass had grown around the tracks, proving that they were left by an object weeks before Bob Taylor's sighting.

AN EPILEPTIC FIT?

However, this did not explain what the witness had seen or what rendered him unconscious. The key was the acrid smell that Taylor reported. Working with a chemist, Campbell carried out tests to produce vials of different odours to try to match the one that the forester had encountered. He concluded: 'It was the result of an epileptic attack. Taylor is not an epileptic, but he had all the symptoms and when I saw his medical history I knew the cause.'

The forester, he discovered, had had meningitis some years before the encounter. On occasions this illness is known to leave parts of the brain susceptible to epileptic attack. He believes that all the physical symptoms described by the witness, including the weakness, inability to speak, headache, strange smells and lack of co-ordination, were a direct result of this temporary storm within the electrical circuits of the brain. Taylor himself, citing the fact that no similar episodes occurred either before the assault or in the fifteen years post this encounter, does not accept this interpretation of events.

JUST A MIRAGE?

Of course, even if it were true, it still does not account for the object seen within the forest. Campbell believes it was an optical illusion, like a mirage in a desert. But caused by what? Putting astronomical data for the date of the sighting into a computer he found that Venus and Mercury were close together on the horizon in the direction in which Bob Taylor was looking.

However, the encounter was at ten o'clock in the morning, when even bright planets are normally quite invisible to the naked eye, let alone visible as a large structured object that filled a clearing. Nevertheless, Campbell claims that the object's size and appearance were distorted by the optical mirage he believes was created by the atmosphere: 'A forester, who has no experience of such phenomena, encounters a very strange astronomical mirage just as he is rounding a corner. It sends him into an epileptic fit because of the shock and he collapses. He thought he saw a spacecraft –

because that was the only logical explanation to him. The ground marks have got nothing to do with it. Case closed.'

In order to prove his thesis, Campbell has checked the details of many of the world's best-known UFO sightings – from lights in the sky to alien abductions – and found that planets or bright stars were nearly always in the same area of sky at the time, even if they were supposedly invisible because it was the middle of the day. By theorising that optical mirages can make stars visible and then distort and magnify them into UFO-like shapes, he speculates that virtually every UFO case may be solved by his new hypothesis.

As for Bonnybridge, he feels that once a lot of reports on one area are received: 'It is easy to conclude that there is something peculiar going on ... But the only thing that may be going on is that there are some UFO enthusiasts in the area, or that the local press have picked up on one of these reports and publicised it. It does not mean that there is anything special about the area ... I doubt that there is.'

UFO WINDOWS: A GEOLOGICAL THEORY

In 1965 American journalist John Keel came up with the concept of 'window areas', speculating about the possibility of a doorway between dimensions through which strange forces might intrude.

Soon afterwards, French UFOlogist Fernand Lagarde published a study indicating that UFO sightings showed a statistical correlation with fault lines – cracks in the rock beneath the earth's surface. Where these faults occurred, abnormally frequent UFO sightings were reported.

Canadian neurophysiologist Dr Michael Persinger used a computer to plot paranormal activity and uncover hotspots. He too found a clear link with fault lines and speculated that energy was released when these were put under strain, as in earthquakes. This energy can cause odd electrical effects in the environment and interact with the human brain, precipitating hallucinations. Persinger also developed the concept of a 'transient', an invisible cloud of energy generated at window areas and floating around the landscape, randomly triggering strange phenomena.

In Britain, paranormal investigator Paul Devereux had found correlations between hotspots and fault lines. He came up with the idea of 'earthlights' as the source of many UFO sightings. His research on geological fault lines predicted that the Pennines should be a hotspot.

At that time there was little collated evidence, but subsequently reports of intense UFO activity have indeed been uncovered and published.

The conclusions of the various experiments that have been conducted into these phenomena, both in the field and in the laboratory, can be summarised as follows. Fault lines inside certain rock types maintain pressure on their crystalline structure and generate an electrical signal in the atmosphere at these sites. Energy may be released rapidly, as a destructive earthquake; at other times it leaks out slowly, as light shows in the sky. The region becomes a latent window. Locations such as quarries (where the rock face is exposed) or reservoirs (where water pressure squeezes the rock harder still) are known to be prime spots for UFO events.

Other factors also seem important, for instance intense sunshine ionising or giving the atmosphere an electrical charge. These features may help turn a latent window into an active window and generate odd auditory effects, electrical surges and other strange phenomena.

Rotating air pockets in the lee of window-area hills could then be charged with this electrical field and create a plasma which glows and resembles a revolving, top-shaped UFO-like object which becomes visible in the sky.

The bandwagon rolls

Steuart Campbell is not alone in questioning the status of Bonnybridge as a UFO window. Even some UFOlogists have had their doubts.

One factor to consider is the way in which the Livingston Development Corporation exploited the worldwide attention focused on their small but fast-expanding community by Bob Taylor's sighting. In the early 1990s the Corporation erected a plaque at the forest site commemorating the encounter. It quickly disappeared (presumably into a terrestrial collection rather than an extraterrestrial one!), but has been replaced. Whilst nobody is doubting the sincerity of the individuals involved, Bob Taylor's experience and the resulting publicity ensured that the embryonic new town development at Livingston became known via UFO books and media sources the

Facing (Above): *A multi-coloured light phenomenon filmed at Hessdalen, Norway*
Facing (Below): *A photograph released from an official government dossier showing an object witnessed above Maspalomas, Gran Canaria*

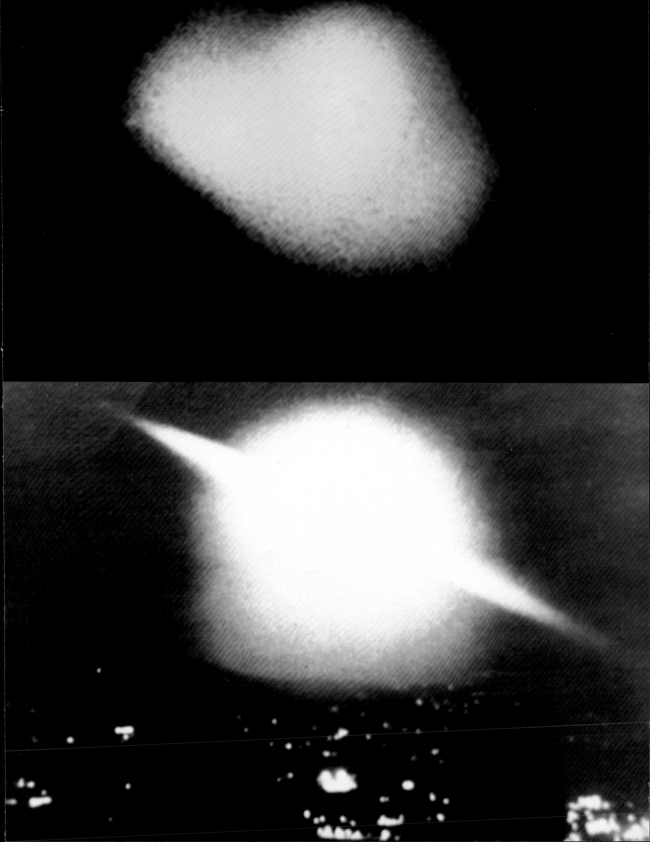

world over. Few would suggest that this was the purpose for trickery or that the episode was hoaxed, but its subsequent publicity value was certainly realised.

There were those who have rather cynically suggested that Billy Buchanan's promotion of the Bonnybridge affair may have owed something to opportunism. This thought surfaced when the Japanese arrived with pipe bands and a UFO-shaped cake. Subsequently a local newspaper reported a doubtless innocent remark by Councillor Buchanan that these visitors might have relatives working for a car manufacturer back in Japan who could come and build a factory locally!

Buchanan answers these charges very fairly: 'It did help boost the economy in dying areas which were destroyed by the demise of heavy industry ... Now I would like somebody from the government to come to Bonnybridge. I have already asked for this.'

So, was a genuine new 'window' discovered in the Bonnybridge area as a result of the extensive promotion? Or were people merely encouraged by the widespread media interest to report sightings at the same high levels that we would find in many other places if similar attention were given?

Facing: *A reconstruction of the events which took place in Rendlesham Forest, Suffolk, in 1980 (see Chapter 10)*

10
OUT OF
THIS WORLD

Astonishing claims are made by UFO witnesses – of strange lights flitting around the sky, communication with other forms of intelligence, even of being abducted by aliens. But none is more remarkable than this.

Credible observers, incredible evidence

In December 1980 perhaps the best case yet recorded took place in a quiet pine forest eight miles east of Ipswich. This close encounter has highly credible observers with impeccable credentials, multiple witnesses trained to watch the skies, devices which recorded what was taking place, physical evidence supposedly left by the UFO, and even an audio recording which captures the experience 'live' in all its chilling detail.

The strange aerial phenomena seen inside Rendlesham Forest in Suffolk, near the twin American air bases of Bentwaters and Woodbridge, have taxed the minds of politicians on both sides of the Atlantic and are officially said to be unexplained by both the British Ministry of Defence and the US Air Force. *Strange But True?* has brought together key participants for the very first time. This chapter contains the most accurate and responsible account yet published of a remarkable story – taking us closer than ever before towards the truth.

The photographs opposite page 129 show a reconstruction of the events of that night.

'Security, this is east gate'

After World War II, the new NATO defence alliance set up military bases in strategic areas. RAF Bentwaters and Woodbridge were two of the airfields leased by the US Air Force from the British government as part of that arrangement. With a British squadron leader acting as liaison officer, the USAF brought over their own men and aircraft.

The two bases were separated by three miles of pine forest and a small road linking the market town of Woodbridge to the coast at Orford. Until their closure in 1993 at the end of the cold war the twin bases served as a maintenance centre for front-line troops in Germany, with the 81st Tactical Fighter Wing operating A-10 'tankbuster' jets and giant transporter helicopters.

A QUIET POSTING?

Getting a posting here was a plum job for American airmen in 1980. You were not in a particularly vulnerable spot, nor did you have to cope with a foreign language or live within a culture far removed from your own. In addition, this was a quiet base. Nothing much was supposed to happen.

At Christmas things were even more low-key than usual, with many activities wound down for the holidays. Airman John Burroughs was on security patrol with a colleague well after midnight, driving near the east gate of Woodbridge, when they saw something in the dense woodland.

'He nudged me and said, "Have you ever seen anything like that before?" I looked back at him and said, "No." I got out of the vehicle and opened up the gate. We proceeded down the end of the road, towards where the forest began. I got out again and saw something very strange – a light in the trees. It gave me a weird, scary feeling ... We decided we had better get back to base and let them know what was going on.'

The first light was dazzling white, underneath which was inset a row of multiple colours all banked up. What they were watching did not seem real – but it was clearly there, pulsating in the cold darkness.

After driving back to the gate, Burroughs phoned the law enforcement office on base: 'Security, this is east gate. We got a problem out here. There's something in the trees – flying out around the base. It's weird. *This is no joke.'*

The last words were spoken insistently, as the desk sergeant was not taking Airman Burroughs seriously – there was a history of jokey camaraderie between the two men. Finally he barked into the phone: 'Listen, I'm being serious. There's something out there. We need someone to come out here fast!'

The truth sank in at last. Via the CSC – Central Security Control – another security unit was ordered to drive out immediately to the edge of Woodbridge base and see what on earth was going on.

John Burroughs

Jim Penniston

A *non-emergency situation*

Sergeant Jim Penniston climbed into his jeep. 'They said there was a non-emergency situation of critical importance ... I guess that meant that it was non-life-threatening. So I did respond, by a code two – which meant lights and sirens.'

He reached east gate unsure of what he expected to find. When he got there Burroughs and his colleague were still staring open-mouthed into the forest, clearly dumbstruck. Penniston saw why. 'The sergeant was pointing to Rendlesham Forest ... I observed multi-coloured lights which appeared to be a fire – the type of lighting you would get with chemicals burning in an air crash.'

'*IT DIDN'T CRASH – IT LANDED!*'

Sergeant Jim Penniston was very familiar with air crashes, having dealt with more than twenty during his time at Bentwaters alone. He was in no doubt that a plane – probably an A-10 – had gone down in the woods and asked Burroughs if there had been a crash. 'It didn't crash,' he replied. 'It landed!'

Perplexed, Penniston phoned control for permission to go into the woods to investigate. He was still going through the air crash check list, ignoring the claims of the two witnesses. Burroughs insisted it could only be a UFO, to which Penniston responded bluntly, 'That's absurd.'

Meanwhile base control checked the radar to see if any 'bogeys' or foreign objects had been detected in the air. Bentwaters tower had picked up something odd about fifteen minutes earlier. They had checked with Eastern

Radar, the main traffic control centre in East Anglia, who had also seen it, as had Heathrow Airport near London. These trackings allowed a plot to be made. The object had come from the north-east and vanished about five miles from Woodbridge base.

An odd blip on the screen

At RAF Watton, south-west of Norwich, where Eastern Radar was located, there was great interest in the strange radar blip. London Air Traffic Control Centre told them that the crew of a passenger jet heading east across Essex had reported seeing a mass of light crossing the sky five hours earlier, at about 9.10pm. Nobody knew what that was (it was subsequently discovered to have been a Soviet satellite burning up as it re-entered the atmosphere).

However, Watton was not the only centre on duty in East Anglia. RAF Neatishead, north-east of Norwich, was active too. Some RAF Phantom jets from another base were in the area at the time, and airspace had been pre-booked to exclude all civilian traffic and avoid any prospect of a collision. So when the unknown target appeared heading into this restricted zone, there was understandable concern and Watton was contacted. They discussed the possibility of a helicopter from a North Sea oil rig, but the blip showed no IFF response – 'identified friend or foe', an electronic signal given off by all civil and military aircraft to provide instant identification.

Mal Scurrah was working the height-finding radar system at Neatishead. He said: 'We didn't know what it was, but we had forty jets in the area. The next obvious thing to do was send two jets in to have a look.'

A FANTASTICALLY FAST GETAWAY

Two Phantoms were ordered in pursuit of the target and Scurrah followed the drama on his screen: 'They got to within about a quarter of a mile of the object and the pilot suddenly started reporting that they could see a very bright light in the sky in front of them.'

Then the UFO vanished upwards and within five minutes had gone out of radar range. The exact height remains classified, as this would reveal details of the equipment's capabilities, but it was phenomenal. Other radar operators monitored its speed as it shot through 100,000 feet. It was doing in excess of 1000 mph.

Scurrah confirms: 'It was stationary on the screen, and then in seconds it moved off at a fantastic rate of speed and it climbed at a fantastic rate as well. There's nothing we had in 1980 – indeed there's nothing we have today – that can perform those kind of manoeuvres. The pilots would not be able to take it.' Radar recordings were subsequently taken away from another base for further examination. The top brass were taking this UFO very seriously.

The object tracked by these radar screens was also seen by human eyes on its route south. At Sudbourne, on the coast near the Sizewell nuclear power station, Gordon Levett was locking up his guard dog for the night when a giant fluorescent white mushroom appeared from the north, hovered briefly overhead and vanished, heading down into Rendlesham Forest.

Although Scurrah is not absolutely certain of the precise date when these events occurred, he is sure that it was around the same time.

Not an aircraft

Back at the Woodbridge east gate, Jim Penniston chose two men – his driver and Burroughs – to go with him into the woods to investigate the matter further. They checked in their weapons at the base – standard procedure before entering civilian land – and then drove along the Forestry Commission track heading into the forest.

Jim Penniston, first to gaze upon the source of the dazzling fire, was stunned by what he saw: 'It started to get a more defined image. I knew at that point in time that this was not an aircraft ... It was not damaged. There was a very bright, pulsating light illuminating the bottom of the craft and there was an extremely bright light on the top with multi-coloured other lights.'

John Burroughs recalls his feelings as he approached the edge of the woods behind Jim Penniston: 'We were trained to deal with almost anything, but no training would pertain to what we were about to encounter.'

Moreover, there was something wrong with the air. 'It was almost like there was static electricity ... like your whole body being charged ... You felt really hot, like your hair was standing up on the back of your head.'

In addition, something indescribable was happening to their senses. Time seemed to have slowed right down to a crawl. They were struggling to move forward physically, as if walking into a barrier of treacle.

Penniston confirms all of this, noting that the charge in the air created 'a slowness with time ... and it took much effort for us to even walk those last 20 feet up to the object'.

An indefinable craft

Burroughs describes how truly fantastic the object was when seen at close quarters: 'There was a transparency involved with it ... But the white light practically blinded you and lit up the whole forest.'

As he and Penniston came to within a few feet of the thing, they were stunned by the nature of what they had encountered. They threw themselves face down on to the ground and, as they graphically phrased it, 'ate dirt'. Without any weapons or any knowledge of whether this thing was hostile in intent they could not afford to take chances.

Penniston, closer than his colleague, also remarked upon the indefinable nature of what they were seeing: 'There were no sharp edges on it. The fabric of the craft seemed like it was moulded and it was black glass. The strange part about the lights was that the black fabric slowly shaded into the colours...' He described it as tank-sized and triangular.

The surface was like smoky glass, offset by the brilliant white light pouring from beneath. The pulsing coloured lights did not behave like flashing aircraft navigation beacons. These swelling shades of colour seemed like part of the function of the craft, as if they were doing something – perhaps even to the stricken airmen. The thing also had three legs in a tripod arrangement on the underside. It was clearly built to make a landing.

A sketch by John Burroughs of the object he saw

AN INSCRIPTION OF SYMBOLS

After they had stared in awe for several minutes in a total, eerie silence, Air Force training took over. Penniston concluded that as they were clearly defenceless targets any enemy would have attacked them before reinforcements arrived. So he got up and moved closer to the object. On its surface, he saw markings.

'It was an inscription of symbols – measuring six inches high and possibly four feet long . . . what fascinated me was that it was on the fabric of the craft, which was sort of like glass – so it would have been like etching.' Penniston could not make these symbols out, but the bottom part was like a triangle and there was a vague familiarity about what he was seeing – almost as if it were some kind of mirror writing.

By now the object had been on the ground for twenty minutes in total and they had been right next to it for two or three of these. Suddenly, as Penniston puts it: 'The craft seemed to move up about two feet and slowly start going back through the tree line. It got about 40 feet away and then it went up 200 feet, hovered for about two or three seconds and then it just shot out of there at extreme speed – faster than any aircraft I have observed.'

As it left in a huge flash of light some cows in the adjacent clearing fled, bellowing. Deer and rabbits scurried out of the trees, oblivious to the humans, seemingly fleeing from the terrifying object. This unexpected rush of natural activity helped to anchor the airmen back into reality.

The search for proof

The officer-in-charge at Woodbridge was already concerned about the men. They had lost radio contact, the control tower had reported lights in the forest, and then there were the radar trackings.

Burroughs and Penniston, however, did not know this; when they were called in, they feared at first that their superior would not believe them.

But he did. They were told to return to the site the next morning to look for evidence. Meanwhile, the officer-in-charge contacted the local Suffolk police, who confirm that they logged a call at 4.11am on 26 December 1980.

SHALLOW INDENTATIONS

David King was one of the two police officers called into the forest to meet with the base law enforcement commander. In the cold darkness there was little to see. Police and USAF vehicles were left on the logging track and the men proceeded a little way on foot. No UFO was visible as they wandered the woods for half an hour. All they saw, as King later noted in the Woodbridge station log, was the beacon from Orford Ness lighthouse on the coast four miles east, its usual sweeping beam blinking periodically through the trees.

Soon after first light Penniston, Burroughs and the officer-in-charge were out in the woods again with several other servicemen, examining the area where they had met the intruder hours before. Very quickly they found what they were looking for – a hole smashed through the top of the pine tree cover as if something heavy had crashed out of the sky, and on the ground three shallow indentations which seemed to match the tripod legs seen on the landed object.

With this dramatic new discovery, Woodbridge police were called back to the woods again.

The rabbit theory

The different police officer who arrived that morning was visibly unimpressed by what he was shown in the forest clearing. He explained – and later entered in the station log – how marks like those were found on the ground in many such areas. Rabbits and hens made them as they burrowed into the earth searching for warmth. He even pointed out rabbit droppings in the indentations.

But the airmen were undaunted by this scepticism. A crew were later brought out from base to measure the pattern of the holes. They formed a perfect equilateral triangle, which was difficult to put down to coincidence.

Penniston notes that the policeman had asked him if he thought a UFO had made the marks on the ground. The airman replied, succinctly: 'I'm not saying it was a UFO. I'm saying it was an object out here in the woods last night and I cannot explain what it was.' In response, Penniston says, the policeman shook his head, saying: 'I'm not putting that in my report.'

As far as the US airmen were concerned, the animal burrow theory was ridiculous. They pointed out that the holes were cylindrical in shape and the ground still frozen hard – the temperature was only 35°F even in daylight. How could rabbits have done such a thing?

The return visit

All holiday celebrations now took a back seat for Sergeant John Burroughs. He says: 'I had a funny feeling . . . I felt it would come back and I couldn't get it out of mind.' It was like an obsession for him. He wanted others to see the thing.

In fact Burroughs was proven right. On the following nights various local civilians and some airmen from the base had seen more strange lights streaking around the sky.

Gerry Harris ran a garage to which many of the airmen took their cars. He recalls coming home from a night out with his wife when he saw some odd balls of light moving in a peculiar fashion around the forest. He watched them for half an hour as they darted up and down, and quickly realised that they were not aircraft – with which, as they lived next door to the airbase, he and his wife were very familiar.

After the holiday weekend men from the base started coming to the garage again, and Gerry asked what had been going on. He was told that it was something they could not discuss, and he says several regular customers were suddenly transferred without warning.

Gerry had driven along the logging track into the forest after he saw the lights. There was a lot of military activity despite the late hour, and some local police out there too. The military police were even armed. After reminding them that this was a public footpath, he was made to turn back.

The top brass investigate

Meanwhile, Lieutenant Colonel Charles Halt, deputy commander of the twin bases, had become aware of the situation. He had eighteen years' US Air Force experience, having served from Vietnam to Japan and come to Bentwaters direct from duty in the Pentagon. He first heard about the affair on the Saturday after Christmas when he checked with the desk sergeant, who laughingly reported what Burroughs and Penniston had claimed to see the day before.

Halt wanted to know why there was nothing in the log book and then insisted that it be properly entered in case accurate details were needed later. He says: 'I knew the individuals concerned personally . . . they were credible. I certainly did not think it was a UFO but thought that something did happen.'

Later that Saturday evening Halt was at a Christmas dinner on Wood-bridge base. The duty security flight lieutenant came in, visibly shaken, and asked to talk to Halt and the base commander alone.

The lieutenant said in hushed tones: 'It's back.'

'What is?'

The two most senior base personnel were told in reply that the UFO had returned to the forest.

Halt gathered a team of four men, including one trained to use a Geiger counter, a base photographer and one of the security men most familiar with the forest itself. He also picked up his office micro-cassette recorder to make it easier to take notes in the darkness. This small team set off into the forest, determined, Halt assures, to 'debunk' the UFO stories.

MASSIVE ELECTRICAL INTERFERENCE

When Halt and his team reached the forest there were already some thirty airmen out there. Generator-operated floodlights, called light-alls, were set up to illuminate the pine forest in the pitch dark, but they malfunctioned strangely. There was some dispute as to whether they were properly fuelled. Later checks proved that they were.

Charles Halt

Halt casually reported this problem on to his tape, noting 'there seems to be some kind of mechanical problem ... gonna send back and get another light-all'. Then he took his men to examine in detail the site where the tripod traces had been uncovered the day before.

Halt has since expressed his relief that he took his tape recorder with him: 'I've been able to sit down and listen to it and go back over the events of that night. I might have had trouble without that tape [as] it's very difficult to believe what really happened.'

The problem with the light-alls continued, even after a replacement unit reached the forest. That there was some kind of electrical field creating this interference is further suggested by the problems the airmen also suffered with their radios. They had them tuned to three different frequencies, all of which were plagued with static and other reception problems that seemed to go beyond those to be expected with dense tree cover.

At the site, Halt recorded notes on to the tape every few minutes, describing the huge hole in the pine tree canopy and the sap oozing out of the trees on the sides, all facing into the 'suspected landing site'. Radiation readings were taken on the counter, with comments like 'This thing's about to freak!' Inside the marks, the indentations and the sap on the pine trees they got the strongest readings – seemingly half a millirem.

The tape records such activities as the careful measuring of the 'pod' marks – as the ground indentations were called – and the taking of samples and photographs to document this work. It all constituted hard evidence that, to this day, has never been released. Halt's team also used a night vision scope to measure emitted thermal energy. This device picked up strange readings of what Halt calls 'heat or some form of energy – it's hardly heat at this stage of the game'.

THE ANIMALS PANIC

Suddenly, pandemonium struck the forest as Halt spoke calmly into the machine: 'Zero one forty-eight (i.e. 1.48 am]... We're hearing very strange sounds out of a farmer's barnyard animals ... very, very active, making an awful lot of noise.'

Halt imposed himself on the chattering voices of airmen placed all around the woods, as many were talking at once. 'You just saw a light – where? Slow down – where?' he barked on to the tape. The recording then recounts the frightening close encounter unfolding in the presence of numerous highly trained Air Force officers.

Like an eye winking

The thing was a reddish sphere somewhere through the trees to the east. Halt says: 'It looked like the sun when it first comes up in the morning; although it had a black centre and it pulsated as though it were an eye winking at you. It appeared to have molten metal dripping off...'

The men watched this spectacle in astonishment, recording their comments on to the tape from time to time whenever Halt had the presence of mind to switch it on. He responded like the assured commander that he was, ordering the men to 'douse flashlights' and to proceed through the woods towards the coast in the hope of catching prime evidence of this incredible thing. They continued to use the night vision scope and the Geiger counter. The UFO appeared to be giving off radiation many times the normal background count.

The animals had by now gone quiet and, as Halt recorded: 'Everything else is just deathly calm... There's no doubt about it, there's some type of strange flashing red light ahead.' Then the thing started to move towards them: 'It's brighter than it has been. It is definitely coming this way... Pieces of it are shooting off! There's no doubt about it – this is weird!'

A SILENT EXPLOSION

The big object moved back over a field that led out towards the coast. Suddenly, as Halt describes, 'with no explanation it literally exploded – but it was a silent explosion'. He added: 'It just disintegrated and broke into three to five objects and it was gone – it disappeared.'

Elsewhere in the woods, according to some of the other airmen, the huge flash had been accompanied by the appearance of a ghostly car-sized object sitting on the ground and riding a cushion of yellowish mist. Some of these men were so stunned that to date they have still not discussed their experience openly.

At this time John Burroughs was near the useless light-alls beside a truck. He saw one of the bluish-white balls of light flash towards him: 'It streaked past the light-all which came on, passed through the open window of the truck, going off into the distance. Then the light-all went out!' It was as if this ball of light was charged with energy that had somehow temporarily powered up the dead light as it passed close by. It was also displaying what seemed to be control.

SPOTLIGHT ON A NATO BASE

Meanwhile, Halt had led his men across the farmer's field from which the cattle had fled on the night of the landing. After wading across a little brook they were now in open land nearer the coast from where there was a better view. They could see more strange lights surrounding the base. Some were like half moons that kept eclipsing, while others moved as if they were performing a map grid search of the area.

Then, as the tape records of one of these: 'Hey! Here he comes from the south. He's coming towards us now ... Now we observe a beam, ah, coming down towards the ground ... This is unreal.'

The beams, like spotlights, were probing the Woodbridge airbase itself. On his radio, Halt could hear the astonished reactions there.

Then a beam struck about ten feet away from Halt and his men. As Halt explained, with this 'we went into shock ... any scepticism I had was gone at this point ... I wasn't sure if it was some type of weapon or some type of reconnaissance ... I didn't know what was coming next.'

After a few seconds, the beam disappeared. But the lights in the sky continued to send down similar 'laser beams' on to the ground.

By now it was past 3.30 am. The men were cold, very tired and emotionally drained by all that had happened. Halt decided to take them back to the base, recording one last message that an object was still hovering over Woodbridge base 'beaming down in this area'.

Dealing with the impossible

So many witnesses had seen UFOs over that Christmas – with sightings on at least three nights and two spectacular close encounters – that being taken seriously was not the problem that it might otherwise have been. Charles Halt reports that he was a little wary of advising his superiors, but knew he would get a fair hearing. They ultimately decided that, as they were guests on British soil, it was the UK's problem to decide what to do with the reports.

Halt approached the British liaison officer, Squadron Leader Donald Moreland, to request the correct procedure. Moreland pondered the matter for some days before advising Halt to draft a memorandum to the British Ministry of Defence. This memo, dated 13 January 1981 – two weeks after the main incidents – was sent by Moreland to London with a covering letter to his bosses in Whitehall. He has steadfastly supported the American officers ever since and says: 'I knew Lieutenant Colonel Halt well. I was convinced and felt that somebody should take notice. Whatever they described could perform feats in the air which no known aircraft is capable of doing.'

UNDERCOVER ACTIVITY

Periodically after that for a couple of months Halt asked, 'Have you heard anything?', but the memo seemed to have vanished into a bureaucratic black hole. But did it?

Other men on the base have referred to special flights that came in and out in the days after the sightings. Halt should have been informed of these, but never was.

John Burroughs speaks of flight activity 'not dealt with in the normal

DEPARTMENT OF THE AIR FORCE

HEADQUARTERS 81ST COMBAT SUPPORT GROUP (USAFE)

APO NEW YORK 09755

REPLY TO
ATTN OF: CD

13 Jan 81

SUBJECT: Unexplained Lights

TO: RAF/CC

1. Early in the morning of 27 Dec 80 (approximately 0300L), two USAF security police patrolmen saw unusual lights outside the back gate at RAF Woodbridge. Thinking an aircraft might have crashed or been forced down, they called for permission to go outside the gate to investigate. The on-duty flight chief responded and allowed three patrolmen to proceed on foot. The individuals reported seeing a strange glowing object in the forest. The object was described as being metalic in appearance and triangular in shape, approximately two to three meters across the base and approximately two meters high. It illuminated the entire forest with a white light. The object itself had a pulsing red light on top and a bank(s) of blue lights underneath. The object was hovering or on legs. As the patrolmen approached the object, it maneuvered through the trees and disappeared. At this time the animals on a nearby farm went into a frenzy. The object was briefly sighted approximately an hour later near the back gate.

2. The next day, three depressions 1 1/2" deep and 7" in diameter were found where the object had been sighted on the ground. The following night (29 Dec 80) the area was checked for radiation. Beta/gamma readings of 0.1 milliroentgens were recorded with peak readings in the three depressions and near the center of the triangle formed by the depressions. A nearby tree had moderate (.05-.07) readings on the side of the tree toward the depressions.

3. Later in the night a red sun-like light was seen through the trees. It moved about and pulsed. At one point it appeared to throw off glowing particles and then broke into five separate white objects and then disappeared. Immediately thereafter, three star-like objects were noticed in the sky, two objects to the north and one to the south, all of which were about 10° off the horizon. The objects moved rapidly in sharp angular movements and displayed red, green and blue lights. The objects to the north appeared to be elliptical through an 8-12 power lens. They then turned to full circles. The objects to the north remained in the sky for an hour or more. The object to the south was visible for two or three hours and beamed down a stream of light from time to time. Numerous individuals, including the undersigned, witnessed the activities in paragraphs 2 and 3.

CHARLES I. HALT, Lt Col, USAF
Deputy Base Commander

fashion', including transporters being 'parked in an area that was not normal and some strange activity [that] went on with the unloading'. Other witnesses on the base referred to a supposedly secret flight carrying photographic evidence to the Ramstein airbase in Germany.

Jim Penniston noticed these odd events as well: 'There were several unscheduled flights that were coming into the air base at that time ... we were briefed that we were supposed to ignore the activity on the Woodbridge side of the base.' It seems that the witnesses were deliberately kept in the dark about what was taking place, having no 'need to know'.

Halt says such stories make him very suspicious, but he insists that there was no cover-up that he personally saw taking place on the base. If one occurred, it was well above that level. He adds that some American agency may have even taken copies of film 'turned into the photo lab' by one of the witnesses. However, no such photographs of the case have yet been made public – despite Halt's tape clearly recording some being taken.

Charles Halt was later promoted to full colonel and base commander, and then given another assignment with increased responsibility, all of which indicates that the authorities did not question his judgement or doubt his credibility. Yet there was a real puzzle about his report. He expected some government follow-up from the US authorities, if not from the British, but 'nobody ever came back and asked for additional information, asked questions, or even interviewed me. It doesn't really add up.'

UFOlogists start probing

Reports about the matter were received by UFOlogists within a few days – even before Halt sent his memo to the MoD. Brenda Butler, a Suffolk paranormal researcher, heard from an airman (who claimed that he was a witness to the events but has never spoken out in public) that a big case had just taken place on base, that airmen were being sworn to secrecy and those considered a security risk reassigned. This man gave her a full account as early as 5 January 1981.

Also in early January, Jenny Randles (one of the authors of this book) heard independently about alleged radar trackings of a UFO made at RAF Watton that same Christmas. An officer there described how two or three days afterwards some US Air Force intelligence agents had come to the base and taken the radar film away – a most unusual procedure, as Watton had no US military presence. In justification the Americans had offered an incredible story to radar staff.

Brenda Butler and a fellow researcher Dot Street turned up at Squadron Leader Donald Moreland's office to discuss the case six weeks after it had happened. At this time there had been no public disclosures and, whilst none of the investigators then knew this fact, Moreland had only sent Halt's memo to the MoD the month before. He and the colonel were anxiously awaiting London's response, so when two women who apparently knew about the case turned up at the base Moreland at first assumed they were official representatives. But he quickly realised that the two women had no jurisdiction and told them he could only talk if they got approval from the MoD. However, he had already said enough to persuade the UFOlogists that the stories they were picking up had some basis in fact.

Jenny Randles, meanwhile, was waging a battle with the MoD to get them to release information. They continued to ignore all requests, until, on 13 April 1983, the relevant department admitted that unidentified lights had indeed been seen outside the Woodbridge base and affirmed in writing that they had no explanation for them. This was an unprecedented revelation.

Armed with this data, American UFOlogists then used their country's Freedom of Information Act to appeal for confirmation. As a result, by June 1983 Jenny Randles had managed to obtain a copy of Charles Halt's memo to the MoD. The US Air Force claimed that they had destroyed their own copy and that this one had been made available by the MoD – the same body that had denied its existence for two and a half years to investigating British citizens.

In August 1983 Randles, Butler and Street presented themselves at the MoD in Whitehall and announced possession of a document 'that may contravene the Official Secrets Act'. After considerable discussion it was admitted by the MoD that the Halt memo was bona fide, that the UFOlogists had come into possession of it by acceptable means and that they could publish it if they chose to do so. Furthermore, the MoD denied (and deny to this day) possessing any more documentation, saying that no other research was ever carried out into the affair because they considered that it had 'no defence significance'. But they will not say how they reached such a conclusion without doing any investigation!

The MOD certainly were not being truthful here. They must have had Squadron Leader Moreland's covering letter, but this is still presumably considered secret as they have declined to release it even thirteen years later.

Mounting evidence of a cover-up

The Halt memo succinctly describes the main events of that dramatic weekend in Rendlesham Forest. Following its publication by UFOlogists, questions were raised in the House of Commons in October 1983 and March 1984 by a NATO defence committee member and Conservative MP, Major Sir Patrick Wall. The Armed Forces Minister gave no direct answers.

However, the case created remarkable interest in influential places. In the USA, Nebraska senator and former state governor James Exon mounted a private investigation on behalf of UFOlogist Ray Boeche. After many months during which he handled all enquiries himself (to the surprise of his staff) and for which he admitted he expended 'more time ... than on any other case since I have been a United States senator', he declined to comment further.

HALLUCINATIONS?

In Britain Ralph Noyes, a former head of the MoD department that receives incoming UFO data, was sufficiently intrigued to make his own investigation and admitted that he felt a cover-up had occurred. He was followed by an even more high-ranking source, Lord Hill-Norton, former admiral of the fleet and chief of staff of the entire ministry.

Hill-Norton discussed the case with UFOlogists then went to the top – to the Defence Minister, Lord Trefgarne. Hill-Norton says: 'Lord Trefgarne is an honourable man, and we knew each other quite well. I am convinced that what he told me was what he believed to be the truth.' Trefgarne had repeated that nothing to concern the defence of the nation was found behind the events in Rendlesham Forest.

Hill-Norton cogently argues: 'Either the Americans, and indeed the deputy base commander, were hallucinating or they believed that something had landed there and they had taken photographs and records of it. In either event it must be of interest to the defence of the United Kingdom. To have American officers hallucinating at a nuclear manned air force base really is extremely alarming.' He adds: 'I had no doubt that, although [Trefgarne] had no knowledge of these matters, somebody in the country certainly did – and it was being concealed.'

SURVEILLANCE, BUGS AND THE 'NEED TO KNOW'

Evidence of this undercover investigation is implied by the feelings of some of the witnesses to these encounters that they were never far from the prying eyes of the intelligence community. Jim Penniston claims that after leaving Bentwaters: 'I had the feeling I was under surveillance and it was at that point in time that I got called in by the air force investigators and requestioned about the incident. They were disturbed that I might say something to the press.' He further alleges that he found a listening device planted in his home.

At the time of the landings Clifford Stone was a US military intelligence officer who came across information about the secret activity following the encounters. He insists that all evidence on the case was sent first to Ramstein air force base in Germany and ultimately on to Washington. The officers who had been involved were considered to have no need to know, and several investigating teams were sent in, each unaware of what the others were doing.

Stone says that a 'finalised report' was compiled in Washington and given a very high security classification. He adds: 'Among the conclusions that were reached by that report was that the objects were real, that there was a technology involved – one that was highly evolved and far more advanced than anything we have – that there was an intelligence behind that technology that we were powerless to do anything other than observe, and that the intelligence behind the events taking place at Bentwaters in late December 1980 did not originate on earth.'

In August 1984 a copy of Halt's tape recording reached the British investigators via a source in the US Air Force. This further demonstrated the significance of the case, giving a 'live' presentation of the second night's encounter.

Since then there has been a steady stream of on-the-record statements by involved airmen, often as they have felt more free to do so after leaving the service. The fact that others have gone public has also helped.

The sceptics' case

There are almost as many theories about what took place in Rendlesham Forest as there are eyewitnesses, although it is significant that neither the British nor the US government has ever backed the sceptics' view. This critical argument is best presented by astronomers John Mason and Ian Ridpath, who contend that a combination of mundane phenomena explain the sightings. They believe that the UFO which initially attracted the attention of the witnesses by the east gate was the re-entry of the rocket used to launch a Russian Cosmos satellite burning up in the atmosphere. Subsequently, disorientated within the forest, they mistook the beam from the Orford Ness lighthouse for a pulsing UFO.

COUNTER-ARGUMENTS

The problem with the Cosmos re-entry is that it occurred several hours before the sightings at the Woodbridge east gate. There was a bright meteor which might have been seen at about the correct time, but only for a few seconds – nothing like long enough for a security team to be called to the gate, drive over from Bentwaters and then set off into the forest and reach a point where the witnesses might have begun to mistake the lighthouse.

The notion of animal burrows as the cause of the ground damage ignores the fact that no rabbits could have been responsible for the huge hole in the pine tree cover 20 feet above ground level. This was seen by all the witnesses and subsequently reported by at least two foresters, who felt that in their expert eyes the damage was unusual.

The radiation levels also seem to have been greater than any left on British soil by the Chernobyl nuclear reactor explosion – something which in 1986 created national concern about the effects on the food chain. Nuclear physicist Alan Bond says of figures reported by Halt and his team: 'Assuming that they had got everything calibrated properly then, according to the tape, they were recording something like twenty-five times the normal background radiation level at its peak ... certainly levels which in the nuclear industry would give cause for concern.'

Bond suggests that Cosmos 749 did re-enter over Britain at just after 9pm on 25 December and that parts had crashed into the forest. 'Whoever in this country knew that had come down quickly cleared it up,' Bond says, and it is possible that what the airmen saw at the east gate was the recovery operation. However, that does not explain what Burroughs and Penniston saw on the ground when they entered the forest.

As to this being the Orford Ness lighthouse, the witnesses say they all knew it was there, had seen it before, and saw it that night to the south of the UFO's position – and that, in any case, no lighthouse can take off, fly around a forest, project spotlight beams at your feet from several miles away, or do any of the extraordinary things recorded by the objects in Rendlesham Forest.

In truth, this remarkable case seems to leave little option but to accept that *something* was encountered – something that, despite the testimonies of the American airmen and such potentially serious incidents at a strategic airbase, fourteen years later remains utterly unidentified.

NEAR DEATH
AND BEYOND

There is one paranormal happening that every reader of this book will confront. We cannot know when or how, but each of us will go through that mysterious process known as death. What we believe happens next – if anything at all – may depend upon our religious convictions. However, we are no longer reliant upon expectation alone. We can use science to tackle the greatest riddle of them all and ask: does anything survive the physical extinction of the body? For a growing number of people the answer to that question would be 'yes'; not because of faith, but as a result of an incredible experience. They have come close to death and escaped, with a memory of something remarkable beyond. Others say they have been saved from oblivion by what they term angelic intervention. Some have even travelled back to claim that this life may not be the first existence they have had. Taken together these stories could suggest that we live and we die, but part of us survives it all – *only* to return to earth and do it all again.

11
LIVING
IN THE PAST

IF THERE is such a thing as life after death, then what of the converse – life before birth? Assuming that we do have an immortal soul with everlasting existence, can eternity mean that we survive only after our death? Or should we imagine that we possessed a spiritual form even before we came to be incarnated at birth?

A widely held belief

This question helps to explain why the concept of reincarnation – or transmigration of the soul as it is sometimes called – has a remarkable hold over most nations on earth. About half the world's population believe that at death – usually after a sojourn in some form of heaven – our soul returns to earth inhabiting a brand-new body. Whilst in most cases this occurs without any memory of past lives, our inner self apparently records a full history of its evolution and there is a learning purpose behind each and every incarnation.

KARMA

The concept of karma expresses this idea best: if we do something wrong in one lifetime, we get a chance to repair the damage another time around. Perhaps we will face similar circumstances and hope to rise to the challenge better, or else we might suffer the sort of fate that our actions meted out on somebody else in a now distant time and place.

Certainly, if karma is a universal rule it is easy to see why conscious memory would be denied to us. The point would be to avoid repetition of our past mistakes through a deeper understanding of moral rights and wrongs, not because at some earlier time we were punished for our misdeeds.

However, even in countries where reincarnation is not a widely accepted doctrine, cases of strange memories do occur. Occasionally they provide some fascinating evidence. But never has there been a story like the one stumbled upon by an American hypnotherapist during what began as a routine session.

'Who is John Daniel Ashford?'

Dr Marge Rieder is a researcher into hypnotic regression from Lake Elsinore in California, a little spa town about sixty miles south-east of Los Angeles. Apart from her routine work trying to help people suffering from phobias or childhood traumas, for twenty years she has been intrigued by claims made by some of her patients that they can recall 'past lives' whilst under hypnosis.

One day in November 1986 Maureen Williamson had a strange experience. She was with some friends in a coffee shop and inexplicably ordered a slice of carrot cake – something she did not like. As she later mulled over this odd decision, Maureen found herself writing the name 'John Daniel Ashford' on to a pad.

Maureen was then a married woman in her mid-thirties who had lived in Lake Elsinore since 1970. She was having regular sessions with Dr Rieder to explore some problematic memories from her youth. Somehow this process of unravelling the past seemed connected with the name that she did not recognise and the sudden choice of a cake that she did not like.

Unsurprisingly, the doctor assumed that this person must be someone from Maureen's childhood – possibly connected with the problems they were trying to work out. So she regressed Maureen and posed the question: 'Who is John Daniel Ashford?' To the hypnotherapist's astonishment, her patient gave a bizarre response: 'He's my husband.'

So the doctor probed further, and that is when a torrent of deeper mysteries poured out. Maureen insisted that she was living in Virginia – a state that in her normal, unhypnotised condition she claimed never to have visited. She was at a town called Marlborough, of which neither she nor Dr Rieder had ever heard. However, the two biggest surprises were Maureen's insistence that her name was really Becky and that the year was 1861.

The search for Becky

The first thing that Maureen Williamson and Marge Rieder did after that hypnosis session was to get out an atlas. They wanted to find Marlborough. 'Becky' had described it as having some hot springs, together with other geographical details, and located it about sixty miles south of a place called Herndon (which a later session revealed was where Becky herself was supposedly born in 1835). The map showed no Marlborough in Virginia. But in approximately the right position there was a small town named Millboro, and Maureen was quickly sure that this was the same place.

USING REGRESSION HYPNOSIS

The use of regression hypnosis was first popularised in the 1950s by American researcher Morey Bernstein, who discovered a subject – socialite Virginia Tighe – speaking as if she were living in Ireland during the eighteenth century. The life of 'Bridey Murphy' was extensively researched. Some facts were proven, but others were not. Speculation abounded that Bridey was a fantasy somehow based on the fact that during Virginia's childhood she had had contact with people of Irish descent. But this was never proven, and the search for more past lives continued.

Most people can be hypnotised, and the level of success has nothing to do with their intelligence. It appears to be more concerned with their visual creativity and capacity to absorb visual imagery. In the state of regression hypnosis the subject relaxes, but does not fall asleep and usually retains full memory of what takes place. The therapist asks questions and images appear in the mind. It is normally impossible for the hypnotised person to know if these are real memories or imaginative fantasies, as both have been proven to occur during the hypnotic state and appear similar in nature when being perceived. It is not common for there to be complete absorption into the unfolding imagery, where the present tense is habitually used and the subject feels as if they are really within the scene that they are observing. However, the richest, and often the most evidential, past life memories do seem to occur when this happens.

Today regression hypnosis is widely used as a method of seeking out such curious memories. However, the reliability of the information that emerges is uneven. Some experiments have provided names and dates that can be verified, while others have no substance to back them up. Either way, there is a problem. When a past life is verifiable, critics can suggest that the source of information was readily available for the person to have read. And when it cannot be confirmed, it can never be established that the whole story was not just a fantasy.

Dr Marge Rieder (left) and Maureen Williamson discover Millboro on the map

As the experiments continued, the correct name for the town rarely surfaced – both 'Millford' and 'Wellborn' were quoted. However, Becky continued to call it Marlborough, even when Millboro was positively identified as the only possible location. This insistence on a false name was eventually to have a fascinating outcome.

In the meantime, the life and times of Becky were explored in a series of hypnosis sessions. A sprightly tomboy with two sisters, she met a man when she was aged just thirteen and went with him to Millboro, where they eventually married. His name was John Daniel Aushlick, although in a subsequent regression it emerged that Becky had always called him Ashford – the pronunciation was apparently very similar. When, much later, no record of even a John Aushlick was traced, but an Andrew Aushlick was found, it was claimed that Andrew was the man's given name but that Becky had always called him John.

'PONY BOY'

According to the hypnosis sessions, John Ashford had a strange upbringing. He was born as 'Pony Boy', the son of an Indian father and a European immigrant mother, at a place called Robin's Nest – not on the map, but reputedly an Indian settlement just outside Millboro during the first half of the nineteenth century. As a young child 'Pony Boy' was smuggled into the town by his mother and given her maiden name as his surname. Few people outside the Indian reservation were aware of his true background and 'John' went on to become Marshal of the town.

Becky lived a fairly routine life. Carrot cake was one of John's favourites, which she often made for him, hence its apparent sudden attraction or her in the late twentieth century. However, back in Millboro, the American Civil War was approaching and the seeds of a tragedy were being sown.

A PAST-LIFE COMMUNITY

Maureen Williamson was a journalist by profession and became determined to discover more about the reality – or falsity – of Becky Ashford. In the third hypnosis session some really amazing ideas were thrown up. Maureen's editor, Barbara Roberts, told Dr Rieder on impulse to ask Becky if Barbara was there in Millboro some 130 years earlier. In response under hypnosis Becky said, 'Oh yes', explaining that Barbara was her mother-in-law. Hypnosis sessions with Barbara were eventually to reveal the missing details of how John Ashford was born and raised in the Indian camp.

A photograph of Millboro taken during the last century

This remarkable new development was, however, only the beginning, for Dr Rieder continued to ask Becky to report if anyone else from 1860s' Millboro was known to her in modern-day California. The reply was 'Yes'. Within months, residents of nineteenth-century Millboro were being identified from today's inhabitants of Lake Elsinore and the surrounding area with astonishing frequency. Some were friends or casual acquaintances, others were strangers to both Maureen Williamson and Barbara Roberts, and one or two even lived outside town, but all had a hand in the unfolding drama.

By 1992 there were thirty-five of them, and by 1994 that number had risen above fifty. This was fast turning into the strangest case of multiple reincarnation ever recorded.

The web of intrigue

One of the first people identified by Maureen Williamson as part of her past-life tapestry was Joe Nazarowski. He ran a private investigation and security company in the same office building in which she worked, and his wife was her friend. Maureen was aware that Joe was a man called 'Charley Morgan' back in Millboro.

Joe only agreed to be put under hypnosis if Dr Rieder could help him give up smoking. When Maureen sat in on the session and heard Joe 'become' Charley and describe the same life in Millboro that she had already done, she was dumbfounded.

Before he was regressed, Joe says he knew nothing of the 1860s' scenario that was emerging in Maureen's hypnotic memory: 'I had no idea of the details. When Maureen talked to me at first about it I wasn't exactly sure what she was talking about. I was one of the most sceptical people, being a retired law enforcement officer. I thought it [what came out under hypnosis] was something made up out of my head.'

But Joe was not to remain sceptical for very long. Details of his 'past life' as Charley tumbled out, and these curious visions or memories wove a perfect pattern with those from Becky, her editor (that is, her past-life mother-in-law) and the various other reborn residents of Millboro (most of whom still continued to call it Marlborough). These people, as soon as they were tracked down, began taking part in Dr Marge Rieder's extraordinary experiment.

THE SECRET AGENT

Joe's first memory was of being wounded at the Battle of Shiloh during the early part of the Civil War. Charley had trained with the Union army and graduated at West Point military academy, having studied along with the future General Custer. Then he apparently switched sides. After being wounded he was posted to Millboro to train horses for the Southern army; his secondary role was as a secret agent, to perform acts of sabotage if the war went badly, for Millboro was of strategic importance.

The town lay at the hub of a rail network with an important tunnel that Charley could destroy if need be. This would block the line and prevent the Union army from using the track to bring in supplies to the major depot there. Although no books on the Civil War have been found which mention the role of the town, and it no longer even has a railroad station, a reference book about the nineteenth-century railways of the area does describe the importance of Millboro as a railhead. Moreover, it noted that the town's name was then Millborough – much closer to the seemingly false spelling that nearly all the past-life residents were still using.

Joe Nazarowski thinks that his fascination with military history in this present life may owe something to his amazing past. He has always been an excellent shot, is a natural horserider, served in Vietnam, but came from Chicago and had never been to Virginia.

He says of his first vision, the noise and smoke of the Shiloh battlefield: 'It was like being there . . . in another time zone or whatever you want to call it. It was very realistic. It was as true as if I am standing here talking with you.'

Although Becky and John's marriage had been a good one, and they had eight children (five of whom survived), there were problems as the war progressed. Because of his Indian past and dislike of slavery, John sympathised with the North and acted as an agent passing information to the Union. Becky, however, firmly supported the South, and secretly began to have an affair with Confederate agent Charley. This was soon to prove disastrous.

'A nice day for a walk, Mrs Ashford'

John Ashford had become aware of Charley's spying activities for the other side in the Civil War, and that he was having an affair. What he did not know was that the woman was Becky, his wife. He made arrangements to end the matter once and for all.

A local villain called Jake Bauer was charged with the responsibility, but seems to have taken his orders to stop the flow of information rather literally. He identified Becky Ashford, did not tell her husband, and on or about 20 January 1865 presented himself at her home as she was doing the laundry in the company of two of her younger children.

'It's a nice day for a walk, Mrs Ashford,' Jake announced, as he greeted the young mother.

DREAMS OF BEING STRANGLED

Maureen Williamson remembers those moments 130 years ago: 'It was a cool day . . . and one of the local fellows – he was just a common thug, I think – had ridden up to the property. He had some contact with Becky then, and asked her would she like to take a walk . . . My feeling in the regression was, no, I don't want to go. He was one of those people paid by both sides of the military to do what was needed to be done. It's possible he was paid to come to the house that day and kill Becky, which he did with his bare hands.' Maureen added that for much of her life she had had dreams of being strangled; this reliving of her own murder was like a catharsis and resolved the puzzle of these recurring nightmares.

HIDDEN IN THE HAYLOFT

One of Becky's children who saw the tragedy has been found and regressed. Today she is a woman named Diana Lovegren. When she entered the experiment she knew none of the key participants and had never met her past-life mother Maureen. Indeed, she was now several years older in this life than the woman who had supposedly given birth to her back in Millboro. Diana was identified as Becky's child by one of the minor players in the story who recognised her (as an acquaintance in modern day Lake Elsinore) during her own regression back to Millboro. This is typical of how many of the smaller characters in the unfolding drama were brought into the study, on the recommendation of an existing member who sensed their identity back in the 1860s, despite their then quite different physical appearance.

As 'Elizabeth Ashford', Diana was able to provide considerable detail about school and home life in the town. She says: 'I knew no details of the story before I was hypnotised. Marge Rieder had asked me if I had read anything about it in the paper, and I had not. I had heard about it and I meant to read up on it, but I never did. I was sceptical, because it's a big story . . . but now I am sure.'

She shivers as she remembers watching her mother being killed in the barn. 'She was a very fierce fighter. I thought she would beat him down, I really, really did. I watched and watched and I could see the dust going all over – and her dress got ripped and she ripped at his clothing and somehow he hit her and she went down.'

Her recollection of this terrible incident went on for many minutes, but Diana was left with one horrible thought – she had been so sure that her mother would deal with her assailant that she had never intervened, not even cried out, just remained hidden in the hayloft. One can understand the powerful legacy of guilt that such images would leave behind.

The hunt for proof

Extraordinary as these interlocking stories seem, they presume the honesty of the witnesses. We only have their word that they had no knowledge about what the others were saying during their own regressions. The first witness, Maureen Williamson, was a reporter who wrote about her memories and published the articles where most of the subsequent claimants could easily have seen them. In individual cases of past-life memories things once read, but forgotten, can trigger a fantasy. Some impressive cases have been con-clusively shown to be nothing more than imagination under hypnosis, built around a novel read or a movie watched years before. The fact that nobody has yet found an easily accessible source of information about Civil War life in Millboro is no proof that such a source does not exist.

However, what is different about this case is the sheer number of people whose stories agree in such incredible detail. They all deny that they are part of some hoax. If they are speaking the truth, this limits the options beyond the realms of reincarnation.

ECHOES OF ENGLAND

Even so, attempts had to be made to verify that the people and places spoken about really existed a century ago. Take the search for Millboro itself. The discovery that it was once called Millborough is important, given the way the witnesses were spelling it. However, perhaps more significant is the frequent reference to the town as Marlborough. Many residents of what is left of Millboro today still pronounce the name as if it were really spelt Marlborough. It is part of Bath County, so clearly this part of Virginia is an area with a strong English heritage. Bath and Marlborough are both country towns not far apart in the English West Country, and it is quite possible that this may be important.

Further evidence of the English heritage pours out of the various hypnosis sessions. Many of the Millboro characters spoke of the outdoor celebrations in early November for 'Guy Fawkes Day' but American citizens would be unfamiliar with the burning of 'guys' on bonfires every 5 November, to commemorate the thwarting of a plot to blow up Parliament in 1605.

Other traces of unexpected affinity to England emerge. For instance Diana Lovegren, as Elizabeth Ashford, spoke of using a 'nappy' to cover Peter, the baby of their family. Americans don't use the word 'nappy'; to them it is a 'diaper'.

EVIDENCE ON THE GROUND

Large-scale maps of Millboro quickly revealed that various small place names given under hypnosis, such as Robin's Nest, were real. However, the true test was to go to Millboro and see what was there today. So, in the spring of 1987 Maureen Williamson, Joe Nazarowski and Dr Marge Rieder spent several days in the town. Each of them was visiting the area for the first time ever – in this lifetime, at least.

So different is the place today that they drove through it without at first recognising where they were. But eventually they began to find familiar locations and one or two original buildings, including a boarding house, which were still standing. The old paintwork of this boarding house was visible beneath the peeling more recent coat, revealing that it had once been exactly as described in the hypnosis sessions.

Then Marge tried an experiment. Independently, she asked Joe and Maureen to pick out the room where Charley and Becky met as lovers. They did.

They also found the railway tunnel and Joe pointed to holes deep within this structure that he, as Charley, bored in 1864. These were set to receive gunpowder charges should the order come to destroy the tunnel.

The Baptist church which Maureen had said was next to Becky's house was white, with a grey stone foundation, a tall spire and a blue window, again as recalled under hypnosis.

Maureen was regressed as she wandered the streets of the town. This enabled her to see Millboro during the Civil War superimposed on the twentieth-century town. The process seemed to create an unusual problem, as the sounds of horses trotting 130 years before made her oblivious to rather faster vehicles speeding towards her down the modern highway!

COVER STORIES?

Nevertheless, the quest to find some record of the real people of 1860s' Millboro has been rather less successful. The team checked local newspapers of the period for reference to Becky's murder, or the subsequent hanging of Jake Bauer, who, the hypnosis sessions claim, was caught. The team also looked at local graveyards. Sadly, the Bath County records were destroyed in a fire in 1909. Nothing came to light that supported the story.

At Salt Lake City, Utah, where the Mormons keep some contemporary census records, Liz Aushlick (mother of Andrew, Becky's husband) was not listed, but an 1850 reference revealed one Eliza Ailstock – which Barbara Roberts then said was indeed her real name. People who recall past lives say it is difficult to hear names phonetically spoken by voices appearing in their

Facing: *A detail from **Descent into the Empyrean** by Hieronymus Bosch (c 1450–1516) showing the classic Near Death Experience of travelling along a tunnel towards 'the light' (see Chapter 12)*

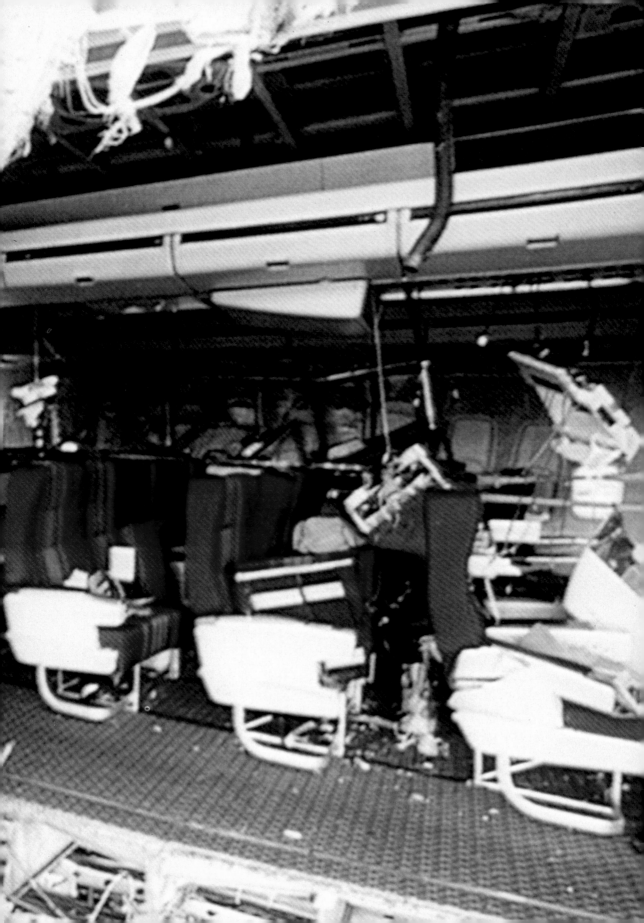

minds, so mistranslation is always possible. Was Eliza Ailstock really the 'Liz Aushlick' who gave birth to 'Andrew Aushlick', who was known as the 'John Ashford' who married Becky and started the whole story off?

There is some support for such an apparently dubious claim. Other records at Salt Lake City show that an Elizabeth Ailstock (about the right age for Becky's daughter, Elizabeth) had existed and married in the town. Also that there was an Andrew Ailstock with a child called Peter and that Andrew's wife died, aged thirty, of unknown causes on 22 January 1867 (two years to the day after the date given for Becky's funeral). However, the wife is listed as Mary Jane Ailstock – not as Becky.

Few details fit, but participants in this drama believe that some facts may have been altered on the records to cover up the tragedy – the year being changed to imply that Becky Ashford (or, that is, Mary Jane Ailstock) died in an epidemic that struck soon after the war was over.

However, perhaps the best hope came in finding Charley Morgan via the records of West Point Military Academy. Plenty of information had been given by Joe Nazarowski under hypnosis to help locate him. Sadly, there was no such Charley Morgan in the archives. Nonetheless, the intrepid researchers found a book about the academy and discovered a picture of one Charles Patterson. This man was listed as being wounded at Shiloh and dying from these wounds in 1862. Joe feels that this man was indeed himself and that his 'death' was a cover story to hide his secret assignment to the town of Millboro – where he adopted the *nom-de-guerre* Charley Morgan.

A new player in the game

Eventually Dr Rieder was herself recognised by one of her subjects as living back in Millboro. She was regressed by another therapist and relived the life of a nurse who had stayed in the area after the war while helping to fight the epidemic that was then sweeping through the region.

After going through several possible names, such as Beulah and Sybil, Dr Rieder settled on Sarah. Subsequently a book was found, written by a Civil War nurse, which mentioned one Sarah Cashman as a colleague. This Sarah had worked in Virginia at about the time in question, and her details matched some of those that Dr Rieder had given.

Facing: *Wreckage of the Boeing 747, flight number 811, from which many passengers had a miraculous escape (see Chapter 13)*

The Marshal's back in town

In 1990 Marge Rieder got the shock of her life when dining at a club in Lake Elsinore. Suddenly she saw a man walk past her wearing cowboy gear. She knew the man – but she also knew without any doubt that he had once, long ago, been John Daniel Ashford.

This man, today Pat Greene, was a very reluctant recruit to the project. It took three years for him to be convinced enough to take part in the experiment – he only agreed in 1993, after Marge Rieder had written a book called *Mission to Millboro*. However, Pat insists that he has not read her book in order to avoid being led by its content.

Various hypnosis sessions have followed and Pat fought hard to persuade himself and the others that what he was describing came from his imagination. But they maintained that he was reporting things that others had already spoken about – including people he did not know and had never met.

Then one day he was shown a photograph of Millboro taken during the last century and he got a feeling about one of the houses – 'sort of like walking up to a roulette table and having a feeling about a number'. He explained that he just 'knew' there was a hidden room beneath it with a trap door leading to an underground tunnel. This was proved when a building which had been on the site was destroyed in a fire. The owner had no knowledge of anything being underground, but when he dug down, he found an underground room and the door leading to the tunnel. Pat Greene was proved correct in every way.

This discovery finally began to dent Pat Greene's scepticism and so in the company of a team from *Strange But True?*, he finally returned to the Virginia town where once he may have been Marshal. As he identified various features and surveyed the now different surroundings Pat said, 'It's like coming back home after you've gone away for a long time. You walk in and everything is very familiar.'

THE SCEPTIC'S VIEWPOINT

What does it all add up to? Do we have a painstakingly researched web of supporting evidence, or has the evidence produced under hypnosis merely been shoehorned into the admittedly rather deficient solid historical data?

Professor Paul Kurtz, who has investigated the case, has no doubt about his views. He says: 'I think Dr Rieder is acting like a novelist or a scriptwriter: she has a plot with characters and the people in her community are taking part in this. I think they find it interesting and exciting. If you go back to Millboro there is no evidence that there was a John Ashford, there is no

(Above) *An old photograph of Millboro in which the boarding house can be seen in the distance.* (Below Left) *Pat Greene in Millboro today.* (Below Right) *The church Maureen Williamson described under hypnosis is still standing*

evidence of Becky who was murdered. There is no record of Charley Morgan in West Point. So the facts do not support the claim.'

He stresses that he is not proposing any kind of deliberate trickery. He feels it is rather like free-form acting or a TV soap opera without a pre-set script. The adventure story is effectively writing itself.

Of course, this reticence is not shared by the participants in this extraordinary story, who consider it to be all too real.

Not imagination

Diana Lovegren (Becky's daughter Elizabeth) says she understands people who feel that this story has all been made up after the hypnosis subjects have read various old books. But she adds: 'If I had made up a story it would have not been like this. In fact, one hundred years ago, from the life I saw when I was under hypnosis, those were terrible days. There were no conveniences. Nothing.'

Joe Nazarowski was persuaded by the discovery of Charley's alleged records and photograph from his West Point days, and the obscurity of the many details revealed in his sessions. No books have been written about, or include a mention of, Millboro in those days. Nothing has been written about the plan to blow up the tunnel. So he is sure he cannot merely be reproducing received information. He feels, too, that there is no way he could have *imagined* so much detail that was subsequently checked out.

Maureen Williamson thinks that reliving the life of Becky (Ashford, Aushlick or Ailstock) has given her many positive advantages. She has become a creative seamstress. She even makes her own soap, using techniques recalled under hypnosis from the days when most women had to do such things just to keep the family afloat. 'The changes have all been for the good,' she says. 'I am a better person for it.' She is now confident that the only explanation that makes sense is that she really was once Becky.

A biological reason?

However, Dr Marge Rieder is not quite certain of that diagnosis. She describes an experiment in which she regressed two sets of identical twins and one set of identical triplets. Each of the twins or triplets relived exactly the same past life as did their brothers or sisters. This amazing finding suggests to the therapist that there is some kind of biological factor at work, too, as all of the siblings were produced from the same fertilised egg and so share the same genetic structure in their current lives. If it were reincarnation, then the soul of a single person from that other past life must have somehow 'split' into two or three to inhabit several genetically linked, but individual, bodies this time around.

Whilst she appears to suspect that a form of reincarnation is also involved, she fears that such emotive, supernatural terms restrict scientists from taking it further.

Explanations

The search for truth about past-life memories is long and difficult. But the argument most often used by sceptics is that of cryptomnesia – the mind's accepted but uncanny ability to record, deep in the subconscious, all things seen and heard right back to babyhood.

PSYCHOLOGICAL ORIGINS?

A number of seemingly genuine past-life memories have been proven to be fantasies made up simply from details of historical records, conversations overheard between relatives and, in a few instances, characters from novels read long ago. This often surfaces in mistakes that are made. For example, a woman recounting a past life in York spoke of the Coppergate area and described gates of copper long ago. In fact the name derives from 'Coopers' Gate'.

Joe Keeton, a therapist who has regressed more people to past-life memories than probably anyone else in Britain, finds that true memories can be readily spotted. People who regress to periods before about the sixteenth century cannot carry on a meaningful conversation with their therapist when under hypnosis, as they cannot understand the modern English language. If when under regression a person from the distant past freely uses the modern idiom or words that are recent in invention, this tends to arouse suspicion.

Another reason to suggest that reincarnation may be essentially psychological in origin concerns the way in which it varies according to the therapist in charge. Joe Keeton, for instance, finds that all his subjects regress to lives within their own cultural group – British people always have past lives in this country, unless they have a different racial background. Yet this pattern has not been duplicated elsewhere with other therapists.

Equally, on average about one in three past lives tend to be of the opposite sex from that of the subject today. However, this finding is far from consistent between researchers – and a significant factor in the Millboro affair is that all of those involved regressed to people who were not only of the same sex, but often with quite similar characteristics.

GENETIC INHERITANCE?

Dr Marge Rieder's research with twins suggests that there may be a genetic memory factor at work. It has been proposed by some researchers that past-life memories are genetically inherited, but how likely is this? Numerous past lives are on record where the person died as a baby or was childless and so passed on no memories to the next generation, unless memory is encoded in some fashion not yet understood, such as through energy fields within the mind.

But one thing is certain. Whatever the real truth, and whether you are a supporter or a sceptic, a story as fascinating as that of Millboro and Maureen Williamson must surely run and run.

12
BACK FROM
THE DEAD

PERHAPS the biggest question that anyone can ask is: what happens to us after we die? In these days of medical miracles, when human life can be snatched back from the brink, or when decisions can be made to keep the brain alive by artificial means alone, this is far more than just an intellectual problem. It poses dilemmas of increasing importance. Indeed – as a result of something fantastic that witnesses claim to be taking place – we may soon *know* if there really is a heaven to which we might aspire.

One man who is certain that some other place exists beyond death is Ron Bell from Dudley on Tyneside. He is convinced that he has died and stood at the doorway to that other world, only to be catapulted back to Earth in great pain.

Ron describes what is called a Near Death Experience (NDE), a phenomenon so well documented that not even sceptics deny that *something* is happening. However, its precise explanation sets in motion an argument that is splitting the scientific and paranormal research communities. Put simply, either cases like Ron Bell's prove once and for all that we possess a soul which lives on after bodily extinction, or they tell us just what it feels like to die – the physical symptoms of those last few moments when a human mind slides into oblivion.

What is an NDE?

NDEs have been claimed throughout history. They are recorded in both the ancient Tibetan and Egyptian Books of the Dead and described by the Greek philosopher Plato. Nowadays, according to statistical studies by psychologists, about one in four people who suffer major traumatic accidents, or undergo surgical operations or resuscitation through heart massage, report an experience of this kind.

An artist's impression of a Near Death Experience

Witnesses relate a remarkably consistent sequence of experiences, commonly reporting a detachment from themselves described as going 'out of the body'. They may even view themselves as if from above, just like looking at a scene on television. All pain is said to have disappeared by this point.

In a few cases the experience goes further still – possibly as the person gets closer to the point of physical death. It is then that they describe a tunnel with a light at the end of it.

Most NDE witnesses who progress as far as the light are desperate to enter because it exudes such a wonderful feeling of peace and happiness, but meet a barrier of some kind. It may be symbolised as a garden, wall, fence or bridge; but however it manifests itself, the person knows that to step beyond means to submit to death. They yearn for death, which they feel sure is just a return to some lost sanctuary. But eventually – perhaps after being given a choice by voices and shadow figures – they decide to return to earth. Then they fly back, at great speed, sucked down the tunnel.

Of course, there may be others who choose to go on. Perhaps they are the victims whom science fails to save – the ones who 'die'.

Ron Bell, fortunately for him and for NDE researchers, was given no choice. He says he was instructed to return when he had his own extraordinary experience.

A fatal slip

That night Ron Bell was in a pensive mood. A few months earlier he and his wife had split up. Ron, having survived two heart attacks, had been forced to give up work; upset and frustrated he became impossible to live with.

But his health was improving, and one evening at around 7pm a friend had given him a lift to take a walk at one of his favourite spots. Ron loved the freshness and the biting sea air of the cliff top paths at Old Hartley, an isolated spot just north of Whitley Bay. It was an excellent place for a bracing walk where you could gaze out upon the North Sea and clear your head to think.

As Ron strolled along the cliff edge he began to feel uncomfortable. A pain was spreading from his shoulder right across his back – he thought he might be having another heart attack. Unfortunately, it struck just as he was standing on the most dangerous part of Hartley cliffs, where the edge is unstable and there is a sheer drop of 60 feet to the boulder-strewn beach. The cliff face is lashed by huge waves.

Before he knew what was happening he was falling against the rock face, trying vainly to grab hold of something. As he hit the rocky ground below Ron felt his jaw shatter, and then he collapsed into unconsciousness.

The next thing Ron knew, he was being swept away by the tide. He could feel no pain, and tried to swim, but then he found he could not move the left side of his body at all.

Ron's mind faded into unconsciousness again, and when he came round the cliffs had receded into the distance. He could not struggle through the sea currents to reach safety. Nobody had been with him, or even nearby when he tumbled over the cliff edge. He was being swept inexorably further out to sea, and death seemed inevitable.

THE MIRACLE LIGHT

Ron drifted in the chilly water, his body numb and all hope fading. He remembers calling out his wife's name and crying hopelessly for his grown-up children.

Then the miracle happened. 'Suddenly, I felt warm and at peace. I was in a shell of misty light. It was not bright. Then I found myself in a tunnel leading off, which was again like mist but with daylight – not pitch black – at the end of the tunnel. I could see a bright light and I started going towards it.' Ron was experiencing the classic symptoms of an NDE – something that he had never heard about at the time of these events.

THE LIGHT AT THE END OF THE TUNNEL

Witnesses' accounts of this scene vary. Some talk about rushing along an avenue of trees towards a sunny glade. In other cases there are descriptions of being 'sucked along the tube of a great telescope' or 'being pulled up into a giant vacuum cleaner'. However, the symbols – presumably forged by the mind to reflect what is happening – are consistent and the tunnel image is the most widely cited of them all.

The light is often reported as being soothing and peaceful, but never harsh or blinding. The person feels drawn to it like a moth to a candle flame, yet there is no fear during this steady progression. There is just a great desire to reach it.

VOICES FROM BEYOND

As Ron Bell glided down the tunnel he found himself surrounded by strangers. He could not see them, but only hear their voices: 'I seemed to be having a conversation with either myself or someone or something. I was being reassured that I would be all right. That I belonged in this place where I was. I felt warm and secure, quite unafraid.'

By now he could see the light growing bigger as he approached it. The voices continued, guiding him onward, coaxing him towards his ultimate destination. Ron was lucid and he knew that this was death – but not some final extinction of all his being. He was heading for a much better place that waited beyond the light.

Silhouetted in front of the glow he could see a peculiar structure looming: 'There was this bridge and all around the side there were shadows, human shadow shapes. They were waving to me, beckoning that I should go on.'

Ron was very calm. He wanted to step on to that bridge, to greet these strangers, who felt friendly to him. But as he tried to clamber on to the steps he was turned back: 'I was told I could not cross the bridge. It was not my time yet. I said I would rather cross, but they said, "No – you must go back." But I felt that I belonged there – this was my way home. Then I was drawn backwards from the tunnel and I woke up in hospital in excruciating pain.'

THE TRANSFORMATION

Ron Bell remembered his experience very clearly when he regained consciousness in his hospital bed. But at first he was confused about exactly where he was.

The medical prognosis had been very poor and Ron had been in a coma for four days after being rescued. At that time of year, with sea temperatures around 6 or 7 degrees Celsius, an average person would not survive much more than two and a half hours in the water. Ron had been in the water for 14

Ron recovering in hospital and able to celebrate a family wedding

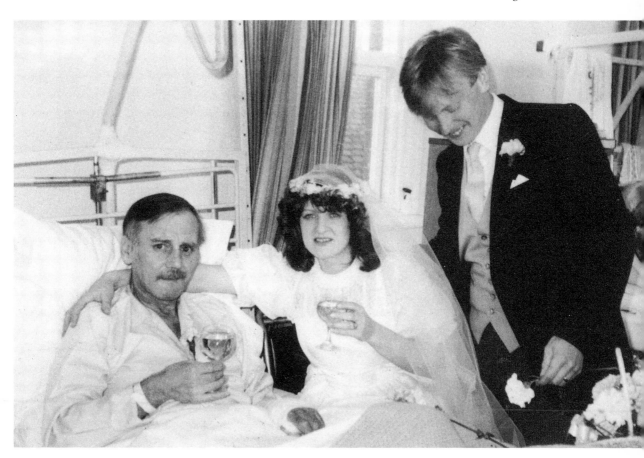

hours, and his body temperature was way below danger level. His injuries included multiple fractures in the pelvis, ribs and jaw bone, and further fractures in his left wrist and left leg.

Dr Sisir Mandal, the consultant physician who saw him when he was first admitted to hospital, said that Ron was very close to death and it was a miracle that he had survived. Carole Quinn, who nursed him during recovery, was amazed that he had pulled through. She remembers as soon as he came round, Ron described his NDE: 'He told me of a dream that he'd had with a tunnel and a light at the end and shapes beckoning. I tended to believe him, because he was very convincing. Indeed, other patients have told me of this same dream.'

The medical staff were not alone in being astonished as Ron made his painful return to health. His wife decided she could not leave him to struggle alone and they were reunited. After seven weeks in hospital Ron was able to go home. But he weighed just six stone, and was confined to a wheelchair for many months. However, he gradually began to fight his way back towards a surprisingly full recovery.

WHAT THE EXPERTS SAY

'The dying patient continues to have a conscious awareness of his environment after being pronounced clinically dead.'
Dr Elisabeth Kubler-Ross, pioneer researcher into medical terminal care

'If experiences of this type are real, they have very profound implications for what every one of us is doing with his life.'
Dr Raymond Moody, medical philosopher and psychiatrist, the first researcher into NDEs

'However the NDE is brought about, the prime purpose of returning to physical life is to gain an opportunity to try to live life in accordance with the knowledge obtained while on the threshold of death.'
Dr Margot Grey, psychologist and British pioneer into NDE investigations

'Most people lose their fear of death ... [After they return] a lot of people feel that they have a mission that they have to go through. There is something for them to do in this life.'
Dr Peter Fenwick, neuropsychiatrist

Ron emerged from the experience a changed man. His family confirm that he became less selfish and displayed great compassion for others – taking an active interest in a local hospice, for example. Ron has no doubt why such a transformation came about: 'I realised that I had been given another chance. But if I was to die tomorrow I would not be afraid. I think I experienced it, and only felt contentment and peace. This is where we all go eventually. I know because I've been there.'

The scientific interpretation

Dr Susan Blackmore, a psychologist at the University of the West of England in Bristol, accepts Ron Bell's story. Indeed, she has heard many similar accounts from people who have come close to death. She even believes that she has had an experience like this herself, which at first she interpreted literally. But she does not do so any more. Dr Blackmore is a sceptic when it comes to the NDE, which she feels certain is perfectly explicable by what she calls her 'dying brain theory'.

She explains that the out-of-body experience is the brain's attempt to make sense of what is going on. It sees its normal self-image falling apart when all outside sensory input disappears. So, instead, it re-creates an outside view of the body, trying to compensate for the changing stimuli.

At the same time the natural defence mechanisms are releasing pain-killers in the form of hormones called endorphins. These deaden the senses and provoke a kind of woozy euphoria.

Moreover, if the brain is being starved of oxygen as the body closes in on death, experiments have shown that brain cells will start to fire in random order. When simulated on a computer screen, this process resembles a bright patch of light surrounded by a dark tunnel.

As for the voices and strange images, these may be simply hallucinations. Many stray inputs come into the brain and may seem more real than they might otherwise do when external stimuli surround or swamp them.

Put together, these elements form a comprehensive solution to what people experience near to death. But, Dr Blackmore says, 'It's not just like dreaming up an imagination for yourself, because it is all being driven by what is happening in the brain.'

Dr Blackmore finds that NDEs are reported even in cases where the person was never in any danger of death – for instance, if they fall into soft snow and walk away unscathed. The *belief* that death may be imminent seems to be enough, suggesting that NDE symptoms are not a trip into an afterlife but are natural reactions to physiological body responses during extreme danger.

As she says, the consistency between NDE cases from all over the world and across the centuries is to be expected: 'These experiences are similar, not because we all go to another world but because we all have similar brains.'

THE DEATH OF HEAVEN?

Has Dr Blackmore destroyed one of mankind's most cherished beliefs, or is there any hope left for the existence of an afterlife? There is some evidence that her seemingly devastating theory has to struggle to embrace, and she herself is prepared to admit that future findings might prove that she is wrong.

THE STAGES OF A NEAR DEATH EXPERIENCE

The main stages of an NDE, as widely reported, indicating in the right-hand column how common medical processes and those factors also uncovered by Dr Susan Blackmore might explain what is taking place in the mind and body.

Witness	*Sceptic*
1. A sense of peace and calm	Natural chemicals released by the body
2. Bodily dissociation/out-of-body state	Mental self-image breaks down
3. Bright light seen	Random firing of brain cells
4. A tunnel into heaven	Illusion caused by motion of firing cells
5. Strange voices	Auditory hallucinations/expectation
6. Heavenly visitors	Visual hallucinations/expectation
7. The border to a land beyond	Symbolised mental fight for survival
8. The choice	Mental decision whether or not to submit to death
9. The return to earth	Medical revival techniques in force

All over the world claims of Near Death Experiences are being actively pursued. Even very young children appear to go through them, lessening the likelihood that such experiences are changed by expectation and adult belief systems.

In one case investigated in 1984 a five-year-old-boy underwent an NDE whilst having a plastic valve inserted into his heart at a Merseyside hospital. As doctors fought to keep him alive, he had an out-of-body vision of the operation. Later the boy was able to describe the object placed into his body, despite the fact that it had never been shown to him or described by his doctors, who had understandably considered him too young to comprehend the treatment. His mother reported that the first words her son spoke as he came round from the anaesthetic were: 'Mummy, why wouldn't the doctors speak to me when I was floating up by the ceiling?'

This kind of naïve innocence, coupled with observation of things that would have been impossible by way of the normal senses, tends to support the view that more than hallucination must be involved. In an incident in Seattle investigated by social worker and researcher Kimberly Clark, a patient who experienced an NDE was able to describe to medical staff a tennis shoe that was out of sight on a high outside window ledge at the hospital. Nobody knew that it was there, but she viewed it in an out-of-body state from mid-air – the only possible way to do so. American cardiologist Dr Michael Sabom, the first medical specialist to study the subject in depth, has also established that NDE patients can describe the complex equipment used to save their lives far more accurately than can others who have only watched TV hospital dramas.

In addition, in at least one of Dr Sabom's cases his instruments recorded that a man who described a full-scale NDE was not suffering from lack of oxygen to the brain. This seemingly knocks out one pillar of Dr Blackmore's theory; however, more evidence of this kind is needed before anybody can be sure.

LANDMARKS IN NDE RESEARCH

Researchers continue to grapple with this fascinating subject. In 1926 Sir William Barrett was the first to attempt the task, compiling accounts from the first three decades of the files of the Society for Psychical Research. They included evidence from dying victims who had been brought back to life and claimed to have had visions of relatives waiting to greet them. Some of these relatives had died only recently and their deaths were not known to the person reporting the NDE.

In November 1967 *Newsweek* magazine carried the extraordinary story of US Army man Jacky Bayne. On 6 June 1966 he had been struck by the debris from multiple rocket and mine explosions in Vietnam and left for dead on the battlefield. He experienced what remains the most horrific NDE, being conscious yet unable to prevent his body being looted and zipped into a bag before being taken to the morgue. He was snatched back to life just as the mortician prepared to inject his veins with embalming fluid.

In 1975 Dr Raymond Moody published *Life after Life*, a collection of NDE stories which established that such experiences were on the increase. This book became a bestseller. In 1977 Connecticut psychologist Dr Kenneth Ring conducted the first systematic study of NDEs and verified Moody's findings. As a result he set up the International Association of Near Death Studies (IANDS). This kept NDEs at the forefront of public debate in the seventies.

The first medical theories were proposed by the sceptics in 1978, suggesting that drugs injected into terminally ill patients were the cause of their visions. But this idea was abandoned when cases emerged where accident victims who had not received drugs still experienced NDEs. Later sceptics argued that it was lack of oxygen to the brain that provoked hallucinations. This was challenged in 1982 by Dr Sabom, who began as a sceptic but was converted when he came across his case of a NDE without oxygen starvation. And a Gallup Poll conducted in the USA in the same year found that up to 8 million people believed they had experienced a NDE.

Dr Melvin Morse published data on very young children who were dying in 1991. Morse was fascinated that 'these children, sometimes as young as two and three years old, use the same description of the light as do spiritual leaders in their description of the light of God'.

In 1992 Kenneth Ring carried out a study of the psychology of NDE victims, which he called the Omega Project. He tentatively proposed that these people were representatives of an evolutionary step forward within human beings – perhaps forerunners of people with extraordinary abilities.

Dr Susan Blackmore launched her 'dying brain' theory in 1993, proposing a range of medical phenomena that might account for all the NDE symptoms in a rational way.

In early 1994 American Betty Eadie published her own account of an NDE in which she entered the light but was then returned, after staying longer than any other previously recorded NDE victim. Her story became a number one bestselling book in the US.

Most recently Dr Peter Fenwick, a neuropsychiatrist from the Maudsley Hospital in London, has joined with a team of medical experts to conduct a test that may either prove or disprove Dr Blackmore's theory.

It involves the establishment of secret equipment and monitoring facilities at various unnamed hospitals. Patients who might experience NDEs at one of these locations will, the researchers hope, either correctly describe whatever might be located there or, of course, fail to do so. The results are pending.

What do NDEs tell us?

The NDE is the most astonishing indication yet of a possible life after death. Instances have been recorded for centuries, but they seem to be more common than ever now that medical science and faster communications are enabling many people to survive injuries that might once have proved fatal.

Of course, amazing as they are, Ron Bell's story and the hundreds of other NDEs on record do not prove that we live on after death, for none of these people actually died. All they show is that, as the end of our life approaches, the human mind seems to experience some quite remarkable and at present inexplicable phenomena.

However, these experiences are not terrifying. They are not even dispiriting. Indeed, they are quite the reverse, and point the way to a hope that there is something more to come.

13
SAVED
BY ANGELS?

THERE is a growing phenomenon sweeping across the world: people who claim encounters with angels. It sounds beyond belief, but intelligent, rational individuals are testifying how their guardian angels have saved them from death, or made dying easier to accept.

Angels of old

According to the Bible, angels were God's first creation, formed out of fire. They make nearly three hundred more Biblical appearances, including angels which foretold Christ's birth and an angel which led Moses to the parting of the Red Sea.

The name comes from the Latin *angelus*, which entered the English language very early. In Hebrew and Greek, it translates as 'messenger', but it is more popularly understood to mean a benevolent supernatural being.

Over the years, angels have been reported to appear in many forms. Contrary to the popular image in church windows and on Christmas cards, Biblical angels were not usually described as having wings; wings were added by artists because angels were able to 'fly'. Daniel (in Daniel, Chapter 10) described his encounter with one while standing on the bank of the River Tigris:

'I lifted up my eyes and looked, and behold, a man clothed in linen, whose loins were girded with gold of Uphaz. His body was like beryl, his face like the appearance of lightning, his eyes like flaming torches, his arms and legs like the gleam of burnished bronze, and the sound of his words like the noise of a multitude. And I, Daniel, alone saw this vision, for the men who were with me did not see the vision, but a great trembling fell upon them, and they fled to hide themselves.'

The popular image of the angel as a winged messenger

Angels played a large role in guiding nations as well as helping and protecting individuals. When Arthur Machen published his story *The Bowmen* on 29 September 1914, it popularised the idea that supernatural beings were looking after British troops fighting in France. The story, which Machen claimed was pure fiction, described how St George and his Agincourt bowmen appeared at Mons and halted the advancing Germans.

A belief evolved that the incident actually occurred. Sceptics have blamed religious and psychic magazines who reproduced the tale as if it were fact. When reports were printed of 'angels' sighted at Mons, this was seen as a transmutation of Machen's story. But recent work by a paranormal researcher, Kevin McClure, has shown that many troops at Mons – British and German – believe they did actually witness 'angels'!

Weeks before Machen published his story, Brigadier General John Charteris wrote home to his family with the information that 'the angel of the Lord on the traditional white horse, clad all in white with flaming sword, faced the advancing Germans and forbade their further progress'. Charteris did not witness it himself, but others, allegedly, had. A few months later the Roman Catholic newspaper, *The Universe*, published an account of the phenomenon from a front line officer.

Bladud: The Bath Society Paper published a soldier's letter in June 1915. He and his comrades decided to make a stand against the advancing Germans, expecting certain death because of the superior number of enemy troops. 'To our wonder we saw between us and the enemy a whole troop of angels. The horses of the Germans turned round, frightened out of their senses. Evidently the horses saw the angels as plainly as we did, and the delay gave us time to reach a place of safety.'

Captured German troops asked who the men on white horses were, thinking they were reinforcements. Many accounts described a peculiar cloud which interposed between the English and German lines. Some witnesses said they could see figures moving around inside it.

While, it seems, Machen's story of St George and the bowmen *was* fiction, it appears to have mirrored actual sightings of angels on white horses who may have saved the lives of hundreds of British troops. And today sightings of angels are once again on the increase. Have the angels returned, as many believe, or is there a more prosaic explanation?

Cliffhanger

Chantal Lakey and her boyfriend, Dale Thompson, had been on holiday in Oregon visiting his cousin. They were driving down from the town of Eugene on their way back to San Diego in California on Highway 101 when Dale stopped the car at a beauty spot he had visited before. The Pacific Ocean lapped at the beach on one side, and on the other rugged wooded cliffs swept towards the sky. At the top of the cliffs, through the trees, Dale said there was a magnificent view. It was an arduous walk, but he wanted to take Chantal there.

Dale was very athletic and Chantal relished the challenge. They began following a path and to her delight eventually reached the top. The view was indeed magnificent: the ocean was all blues and greys, and behind them stretched an emerald-green forest.

After a while they decided to start back down, but part way Dale came across another path near the cliff edge, which seemed to lead down to the beach. He suggested they follow it. After a few feet, however, the path fell away and they found themselves on a narrow ledge. The rock was like shale and very loose, and when they tried to climb back up, it just slipped away. So they decided to inch their way down.

Dale moved first, but whenever Chantal tried to follow she sent a shower of debris over his head. He went down a few feet more until he was balanced on a tiny ledge, and put out his hands to help her. Chantal will never forget what followed.

'I was terrorised, scared to death. I was just so afraid. At that moment, with his hand reaching out for me, he looked into my eyes and fell backwards. His foot slipped out from under him and I saw him hit a ledge, and he kept falling until I couldn't see him any more. I was up there all alone and I screamed his name. I screamed *Dale*!'

THOUSANDS OF VOICES

Chantal knew that if she moved it would be the end. Yet she had to get down and find help for her boyfriend. She shouted for ages, but the only reply was the crashing of the ocean. No one even knew they were there. Even though Chantal was an agnostic, she turned to God for help. 'I felt this over-whelming urge to call God's name. At that moment I heard a soft choral

Doré's engraving of angels captures the 'mist of angels' impression that Chantal Lakey experienced

sound, a wonderful soothing singing. Yet I was still terrified. The voices became very gentle and this gave me some comfort and peace. Then my eyes seemed to go out of focus and I was in a mist surrounded by angels.'

There were too many to count, and Chantal found difficulty focusing clearly on any one of them. They just kept singing, soothing her and encouraging her to climb down and get help for Dale. 'In that instant I knew there was God and I knew there were angels. I started moving, but don't remember climbing down the first three hundred feet. I feel they floated me down somehow. When I started the final two hundred feet I lost my footing and started falling. I remember feeling this gigantic hand swooping down and grabbing my body and pushing me up against the rock.'

Chantal made it to the beach, and the whole time the angels kept singing. 'There's nothing to describe that sound, it's like thousands of voices.'

She found Dale on the beach. He was dead. But Chantal says she knew the angels had not deserted him. 'I knew that he was with the angels. Not only had they helped me down from the cliff, they were assisting him in his death.'

When a rescue team finally arrived they found it impossible to get down the cliff face, even though several were experienced mountain climbers. Dale's body was retrieved by helicopter.

Mark Metcalf, the police lieutenant who attended the scene, said: 'It's the opinion of the rescue personnel that once committed, neither could a person come down unassisted, nor go back up. So how she got off that rock is left to speculation.'

Chantal did finally marry after spending years getting over the trauma. She believes the angels brought her and her husband, Andy, together. 'We discovered our lives had been paralleling each other for years. His sister was born in the same hospital as my brother, as children we lived in the same town, then we both moved to San Diego and we worked at the same post office.' Perhaps most amazing of all, Chantal discovered that Andy had also had an angel experience. He claims they had saved his life too.

Dead certain

Unlike Chantal Lakey, Marilynn Webber had been brought up to believe in angels. The first time an angel saved her life was while she was a student in Chicago. Her parents lived in the suburbs, and she would take the train to visit them at weekends. On this particular weekend Marilynn was distressed after hearing the news that her Sunday school teacher was terminally ill.

When she got off the train, Marilynn was deep in thought. She began walking across the railway lines.

'I looked up and saw a train almost on top of me, and when I tried to move

I was frozen with fear. I knew in those few seconds I was going to die. The one thing that ran through my mind was that I was going to be in Heaven before my Sunday school teacher. Just before the train was about to run over me, I was pushed from behind with a tremendous force that sent me flying off the tracks and down the siding.'

When Marilynn climbed back up to the tracks she looked for the person who had saved her, but there was no one in sight. She was convinced it must have been her guardian angel. Marilynn prayed that one day she would see an angel. But when this happened, in August 1993, it was not as she expected.

ANGELS IN BLACK

'I had a dream that was different from any other dream I'd experienced. There were four angels – but they weren't the angels that I wanted to see, beautiful and glorious – they were dressed in black robes. Summoning up courage, I asked the angel on my right why they looked so sad. The angel said: "We're sad because you're dying. Unless something is done you will die."'

She woke up in a cold sweat with a terrible pain in her abdomen and told her husband about the dream. The next morning, they went to a hospital where Marilyn was diagnosed as having cancer of the uterus. An immediate hysterectomy was advised. Marilynn expected to be in intensive care and hospitalised for some time, but went home five days after surgery. The doctors were amazed.

They went on to tell her that with the type of cancer she had, she would normally have felt no pain until the cancer was too advanced for surgery. Marilynn believes that the pain she felt at this early stage was a further reinforcement from the angels for her to see a doctor. The surgery was so successful that she did not need chemotherapy. She said: 'Had it not been for the angels, I wouldn't have been to the doctor even yet. They weren't the angels I wanted to see, but they were the angels who saved my life.'

The hospital confirmed their part in this unusual story.

Angels on flight

On 24 February 1985 Shari Peterson was flying between Denver, Colorado and Auckland, New Zealand. It was something she was well used to, having to fly often in her job as a travel guide. The Boeing 747 stopped in Honolulu, Hawaii to refuel and Shari was upgraded from the back of the plane to row 13. On reboarding, something seemed odd.

'When you fly you don't really look at anyone else, you're in your own little world. But as the flight attendant walked towards me we looked at one another and she gave me a big smile and a knowing look. I began looking at all the people around me as if I needed to notice them for some reason. I made some sort of contact which is something I never normally do.'

Flight 811 took off at about 1am from Honolulu. Once at cruising altitude Shari loosened her safety belt, reclined the seat and began reading a book. She was engrossed in the story when suddenly a loud voice broke into her concentration. *Tighten your seat belt.*

Shari twisted round to see who had spoken, but there was no one there. She went back to her book, then began thinking about what had been said. *That's not what one person would say to another*, she thought. So Shari decided there was nothing to lose in tightening up her seat belt. After doing so she lay back and relaxed. Within sixty seconds there was a 'pop' and sudden decompression. Shari was yanked forward and she opened her eyes.

DISASTER FIVE MILES HIGH

'The whole side of the aircraft was gone, including rows eight to twelve. The gentleman sitting next to me was perched at a thirty degree angle, his feet bouncing in the aisle. The floor was gone, the seats were gone, including the people sitting in them. A gentleman sitting on the arm seat was blown out of his seat, across the aisle to his death. The interior was reduced to a shell – that's how strong the decompression was.'

Almost two years later the United States Navy recovered the cargo door from thousands of feet below the Pacific Ocean. Investigators concluded that an electrical short circuit had opened the door in flight. The 300 knot airstream had ripped it back, creating a hole, 15 by 20 feet, in the fuselage.

'The hostess who had made eye contact with me was wedged under my seat, and I was holding on to her. I could see couples talking but you couldn't hear anything. There was a flight attendant with a megaphone yelling, but the engines were real loud and the wind was rushing past. At that point we were five miles up and doing 400 miles a hour.'

Sparks pierced the darkness as bare electrical wires touched one another or the exposed framework of the aircraft.

'I closed my eyes again, and I'm thinking, *Whoever told me to tighten up my belt, please help.* I pictured in my mind a big hand coming in under the airplane and holding it up until we landed back at Honolulu.'

Afterwards, Shari became acquainted with the pilot, Captain Cronin. Two engines had caught fire and the aircraft was heavy with fuel – basically just falling out of the sky. 'He said he did not land that airplane, I quote.' Computer simulations of the accident were later unable to show how the plane could have landed.

Shari Peterson is convinced that 'a messenger from somewhere . . . I believe it was an angel' saved her life – but, as emerged later, she was not the only passenger to hear a disembodied voice.

The wreckage of the Boeing 747

Bruce Lampert is a former pilot who earns his living as a lawyer specialising in injury claims for the victims of aircraft disasters. As he boarded Flight 811 Lampert never suspected he was about to become a victim himself. Later he represented about fifty passengers in claims against United Airlines and the Boeing Aircraft Company. It was while taking statements that he first learned about Shari's experience, and that of another passenger too. A husband who was clinging on to his wife in a life or death struggle suddenly heard a voice which said: *Sir, it's not your time. Relax, it's going to be OK. You're going to be all right.*

Bruce Lampert has been involved with almost every major American aircraft disaster in recent years. In his professional view, everyone should have perished on Flight 811. Of Shari Peterson, he said: 'She was directly opposite the hole in the main deck. If Shari had not been "warned" to fasten her seat belt, she would have been an additional death.'

The sceptical view

Should we accept the testimonies of people like Chantal Lakey, Marilynn Webber and Shari Peterson at face value? What other explanations are there? Why believe in mythical creatures when the real source for these experiences might be nearer home than in heaven?

Barry Beyerstein is a professor who studies brain behaviour in the department of pyschology at the Simon Fraser University in Canada. He views the whole upsurge in angel encounters with cynicism.

'One of the bestsellers on the *New York Times* list has been a book on angels. There are now mugs, hats and shirts bearing angels, and anything else the mass market can dream up to cash in on this new fad.'

But what about the people who are claiming to have the experiences?

'There are people who are clearly deranged and have hallucinations. But the interesting people, the ones responsible for the trend, are by and large as normal as anyone else. That's what's so fascinating about the phenomenon. We tend to think of people who have strange visions as either liars, fools or mentally ill, and that's not necessarily the case. I don't doubt them for one minute.'

BRAIN-PRODUCED IMAGES

Professor Beyerstein believes the experiences are a response by the brain to threats of danger. They are subjective visions and do not exist in the outside 'real' world.

'Our brains are capable of producing images in daydreams, nightdreams and fantasies all the time, and generally we don't mistake them for real perceptions. But one of the things that the science of neurology tells us is that the same mechanisms of the brain that process information coming in through the eyes also process information coming from our memory banks.'

Beyerstein feels that when this happens during a time of stress people are unable to tell that the information they are receiving is actually from an internal source and not an external one. The cosmetic appearance of the vision depends on their hopes, fears, education, past experiences and culture.

'Whether they interpret that as an angel, demon or a fairy is largely culturally determined. At this particular time our culture says it is OK to interpret them as angels. A competitor to this is the alien. Perhaps those with a technological bent see it not in a traditional religious context, but something more hi-tech – something from another galaxy rather than from heaven.'

PREMONITIONS IN THE SUBCONSCIOUS

But how can angels be triggered off *in advance* of a life-threatening situation? Professor Beyerstein thinks he has the answer to that too.

'In many cases we sense danger on a subconscious level. Something on the periphery of our vision or hearing that we are not consciously paying attention to. For instance, the smell of an engine overheating. Deep down something is saying: *We really ought to do something to protect ourselves*. For some people it will come as a direct thought. For others it will be a vague intuition. Then there are people who will experience a visual or auditory message. But it is still coming from *us*. One part of the brain is warning another.'

Beyerstein speculates that the brain would conjure up the image of an angel to have a calming effect on the individual, preventing them from panicking and doing something counter-productive. As far as he is concerned, angels do not have an objective existence.

Non-Christian witnesses

The explanation put forward by Barry Beyerstein for angels is attractive, and in many ways it makes sense – but only up to a point. There was no warning that the cargo door on flight 811 was about to fly open, for instance, no tell-tale smell of 'burning' detected by Shari Peterson's subconscious mind. And why should agnostics or followers of non-Christian religions 'conjure up' angels? Vicki Stafford who lives in Sussex awoke one night in 1991 and looked outside. There, kneeling in the garden as if in prayer, was a fair-haired man with wings. Vicki is a Buddhist.

The testimony of companions

Professor Beyerstein believes that such sightings take place only 'in the theatre of the mind'. If that is the case, how does it explain incidents with more than one witness? Well-known healer Soozie Holbeche lost control of her car in appalling weather and went into a skid. Then she felt a cool breeze on her face and someone else seemed to take hold of the steering wheel and straighten the car up. Soozie had two more angel experiences, and during the second she says there was someone with her. She was chatting to a male friend at work when a wave of heat seemed to burn through her. The friend stepped back with a look of astonishment on his face. Suddenly Soozie's temperature was back to normal. Her friend shook his head in disbelief. 'Behind you,' he blurted, 'I saw an angel.'

'SOMEONE' AT THE WHEEL

Angels can appear in a number of guises. But they usually arrive at a moment of peril and disappear afterwards.

Pam Fardon and her husband Ray were running a youth camp in Devon in the late 1960s. Suddenly one day they saw a tractor careering down a hill. It was being driven by a man wearing a brown smock. The couple were full of admiration for the driver's skill as he managed to avoid people picnicking on the grass. At the last moment the tractor turned, just missing a car park, and went over a cliff on to a busy road below.

Ray ran down to the cliff edge, expecting to find people dead and injured. But the tractor had only fallen on to a parked car. Just moments earlier a woman in the car had climbed out and walked away without knowing why. Ray climbed down and searched through the wreckage for the driver of the tractor, but no one was there.

They discovered that no one had been on the tractor when it careered down the hill. The driver had climbed off the vehicle to shut a gate, and left the engine running. Before he could get back to the tractor it had begun rolling away. Pam and Ray know there would have been many deaths and injuries but for the hand of someone at the wheel. 'Someone' they had both seen.

THE GUARDIAN ANGEL

Melissa Deal Forth, the manager of a large country and western night club, was married to a Nashville musician-songwriter, Chris Deal, who played in bands and did session work for major artists. In 1980 Chris started coming home very tired, which was odd because he was so fit. Melissa wanted him to visit a doctor, but he put it off because it was Christmas and he was very busy. In January 1981 he finally went for an examination and was diagnosed as suffering from acute lymphatic leukaemia.

At that time bone marrow transplants were only very experimental, but a perfect match was found in Chris's brother. Chris was sent to a cancer hospital called MD Anderson in Houston, Texas, and given chemotherapy to get him into remission before the transplant. After seven months the illness and drugs had transformed this tall, well-built man into an under-weight, weak shadow of himself, who spent most of his time in a heavy state of depression, sleeping and waiting to die.

Melissa stayed with him in the hospital. Usually she was up and down all night attending to him – if so much as a pin dropped it would wake her. This particular night what woke her was a frantic nurse telling her that Chris had disappeared. He was so ill he could barely walk, and he was hooked up to an intravenous system. But he was gone, and had managed to walk past the nurses' desk to the door without being seen.

Melissa went barefoot out into the corridor looking for her husband. Eventually she found him in the chapel, kneeling, almost touching knees with another man.

BLUE JEANS AND ICE-BLUE EYES

This was three o'clock in the morning, and all relatives in the building had an identification number and could only get on to their own floor with a pass. Melissa knew all the family members on the floor, and he was not one of them.

'I looked at this guy and was afraid he might be dangerous,' she recalled. 'His skin was so white and flawless it was almost transparent. There was not a wrinkle on him. When I walked in he looked down at the floor and I looked down. He wore blue jeans, a flannel shirt and boots – the attire that Chris normally wore – but these clothes looked like they'd just come off the rack. In retrospect, I feel he was attired in Chris's clothes to make him feel more relaxed.

'I was trying to persuade Chris to come back to the room, but he kept asking me to "please go". At this point the young man looked up at me. He really only looked like a youth of fifteen or sixteen. He had two most unbelievable brilliant ice-blue eyes. Immediately I knew everything was OK. It was a very strange feeling in there, as if time stood still. So I walked out and shut the door.'

She returned to the room and told the staff that she had found Chris and he was all right. Then she sat on the edge of his bed for half an hour awaiting his return. When he appeared, dragging the intravenous pole, he looked trans-formed. He was grinning from ear to ear.

'I knew immediately something had happened. Physically you could still tell he had gone through the wear and tear of chemotherapy, but there was something about his spirit which had changed. His energy was back and he no longer looked like a man carrying a terminal illness.'

Melissa could not contain herself and bombarded her husband with questions about the strange young man. Who was he? Where had he come from? What was he doing with her husband? Chris went very serious, and said: 'You're not going to believe me.' Then he explained that the man was an angel – his guardian angel.

An unbelievable transformation

Melissa ran back to the chapel, which was now empty, then stepped into a lift and went down to the main floor. There she found a security guard and described the stranger. The guard said that no one of that description had passed him.

'I went back up to Chris's room and said I couldn't find him, but maybe he'd got off on another floor. Chris thought that was kind of funny.'

The angel had told Chris that Melissa had been put into a deep sleep then he had been summoned to the chapel. Chris had entered and went down on his knees praying. Then he heard a voice behind him. 'Are you Chris Deal?' Chris turned round and there was the young man, who added: 'I've come to help you.' During their deep conversation, the angel told him that his prayers had been answered. It was a non-denominational chapel and Chris never told him he was a Roman Catholic. But the angel asked him if he wanted to say the Rosary.

'The transformation in him was unbelievable,' says Melissa. 'You've got to understand that here was a man who couldn't walk by himself. I thought he had been healed. From the time the angel came, everything changed. He started eating again, he was up visiting the other patients and laughing. Two days later he died, peacefully and without fear. The angel had come to help him die.'

The experience had a long-term effect on Melissa. 'Now I know there's something that takes care of us. It has changed my life. I'm not even close to the same person I used to be. We were rock-and-rollers, living a wild lifestyle. Angels to us meant mythical creatures that appeared on Christmas cards. If someone had come up to me and said: "That guy over there is an angel", I would have thought: *This person is not working on all tracks*. But I'll never forget that flawless skin and those clear, ice-blue eyes. When you come face to face with an angel you never, ever, doubt again.'

BIBLIOGRAPHY

Blackmore, Susan *Dying to Live* (Grafton 1993)

Butler, Brenda, Street, Dot & Randles, Jenny *Sky Crash* (Grafton 1986)

Campbell, Steuart *The UFO Mystery: Solved!* (Explicit 1994)

Cavendish, Richard (Editor) *Man, Myth & Magic* Part-work (Purnell 1970–72)

Cavendish, Richard (Editor) *Encyclopedia of the Unexplained* (Routledge & Kegan Paul 1974)

Cheetham, Erica *Prophecies of Nostradamus* (Corgi 1973)

Cockell, Jenny *Yesterday's Children* (Piatkus 1993)

Cracknell, Bob *Clues to the Unknown* (Hamlyn 1981)

Devereux, Paul (et al) *Earthlights Revolution* (Blandford 1989)

Fairley, John & Welfare, Simon *Arthur C. Clarke's Chronicles of the Strange and Mysterious* (Collins 1987)

Fawcett, Larry & Greenwood, Barry *Clear Intent* (Prentice-Hall 1984)

Grant, John *Dreamers* (Ashgrove 1984)

Harris, Melvin *Sorry You've Been Duped!* (Weidenfeld & Nicolson 1986)

Hodgkinson, Liz *Spiritual Healing* (Piatkus 1992)

Hough, Peter & Randles, Jenny *The Complete Book of UFOs* (Piatkus 1994)

Jones, Nella *Nella: A Psychic Eye* (Ebury Press 1992)

McClure, Kevin *Visions of Bowmen and Angels* (self-published booklet available from 42 Victoria Road, Mount Charles, St Austell, Cornwall PL25 4QD)

Moody, Ray *Life After Life* (Bantam 1975)

Morse, Melvin *Closer to the Light* (Souvenir 1990)

Price, Harry *The End of Borley Rectory* (Harrap 1947)

Randles, Jenny *From Out of the Blue* (Berkley 1993)

Randles, Jenny *Time Travel* (Blandford 1994)

Randles, Jenny *UFOs and How to See Them* (Anaya 1992)

Randles, Jenny & Hough, Peter *The Afterlife* (Piatkus 1993)

Randles, Jenny & Hough, Peter *Death by Supernatural Causes?* (Grafton 1988)

Randles, Jenny & Hough, Peter *The Encyclopedia of the Unexplained* (Michael O'Mara 1995)

Reider, Marge *Mission to Milboro* (Blue Dophin 1993)

Ring, Kenneth *The Omega Project* (William Morrow 1992)

Rogo, D. Scott *The Poltergeist Experience* (Aquarian Press 1990)

Underwood, Peter *This Haunted Isle* (Javelin 1986)

Watson, Lyall *Supernature* (Coronet 1974)

Watson, Lyall *Beyond Supernature* (Hodder & Stoughton 1986)

Wilson, Ian *Mind Out of Time* (Gollancz 1981)

Wood, Robert *The Widow of Borley* (Duckworth 1992)

Zohar, Dinah *Through the Time Barrier* (Heinemann 1982)

ABOUT THE AUTHORS

Jenny Randles is an established writer, broadcaster and expert on the paranormal and UFOs. She has written and presented programmes for both television and radio, and regularly lectures around the world. Her work has included briefing senior British politicians at Westminster on UFOs. She is a member of BUFORA, the British UFO Research Association and for twelve years was their Director of Investigations. She continues to operate BUFORA's news and information service. Jenny Randles is the author of over 20 books and is currently working on *The Paranormal Source Book* (Piatkus). She lives on Lancashire's Fylde coast.

Peter Hough is a well-known researcher into the paranormal and has lectured widely on the subject. He has taken part in many television and radio broadcasts and has acted as consultant and contributor to television documentaries. He has written several books and numerous articles, and is currently working on *Supernatural Britain: A Guide to Britain's Most Haunted Places* (Piatkus). Peter Hough is a member of the Association for the Scientific Study of Anomalous Phenomena (ASSAP) and he lives near Warrington, Cheshire.

Jenny Randles and Peter Hough were consultants to the LWT series *Strange But True?* and are co-authors of *The Afterlife: An Investigation into the Mysteries of Life After Death* and *The Complete Book of UFOs: An Investigation into Alien Contacts and Encounters*, both published by Piatkus.